WHY WOM

WHY WOMEN DON'T HAVE WIVES

Professional Success and Motherhood

Terri Apter

First published 1985

Published by
THE MACMILLAN PRESS LTD
Houndmills, Basingstoke, Hampshire RG21 2XS
and London
Companies and representatives
throughout the world

Printed and bound in Great Britain by
Anchor Brendon Ltd, Tiptree, Essex

British Library Cataloguing in Publication Data
Apter, T.E.
Why women don't have wives.
1. Women—Employment
I. Title
305.4′3   HD6053
ISBN 0–333–35450–8
ISBN 0–333–35451–6 Pbk

To my two mothers

Contents

Acknowledgements   viii
Foreword   ix
1 What do Women Want?   1
2 Why do Women Mother?   11
3 What do the Children Need?   45
4 Why Women Fail   61
5 Depression – A Female Ailment?   72
6 New Options – Having It All   84
7 The Wage Learners:
   Working as Necessity   104
8 Star Performers   122
9 Dressed for Success   138
10 Fitting It In –
   Part Timers and Late Bloomers   159
11 Looking Ahead   179
Notes and References   185
Selected Bibliography   189
Index   193

ACKNOWLEDGEMENTS

I wish to thank all the women who spoke to me or wrote about their lives as working mothers. As they create their lives, they are creating the future for all women, and therefore my thanks goes beyond their help with this book.

I have used pseudonyms for those women who requested it, and these have been indicated with an asterisk; but because the particular details of their lives are precisely what make them interesting, I have changed as little of these as possible.

From the earliest stages of writing I benefited from discussions with Anne-Lucie Norton of Macmillan Press. I am grateful for her continuing interest and encouragement.

FOREWORD

This book grew out of my curiosity as to the practical and psychological effects on women today of the high ideals of the 1970s. More women were working. More women valued financial independence. More women were stimulated to respond to a wider range of needs. More women were focusing career ambition upon themselves, rather than on their husbands and children. Yet women were still mothers, and motherhood was not changing.

Motherhood has always been a poor relation among feminist topics. Initially it was thought that motherhood would be radically changed. The only thing that did change was that women saw they could not expect total fulfilment from motherhood. Their expectations of motherhood were decreased, but this did not decrease the amount of work motherhood involved.

Certainly the working mothers of today are more demanding of the fathers. Certainly the father plays a larger role in child care. And we are encouraging him to feel more involved. His participation in the birth itself may encourage an active bond between the father and the infant. Since men and women are equal, will the father not feel what the mother feels when he holds his new child? It has been assumed this will be so, but the advances in paternal care are slow, piecemeal, full of reminders, arguments and disappointments. 'Mothering' a child still means something very different from 'fathering' a child. A woman who succeeds in a career and who is also a parent, therefore, does not combine these roles as a man does, and faces an entirely different set of problems.

Because motherhood refused to change while everything else to do with women was changing, women's special suitability as mothers became an enticing study. Explanations as to why women were particularly good at mothering, and why they continued to mother, were advanced from every angle – moral, psychological, evolutionary. Women, it was found, spoke a different moral language. They thought in terms of concern for others, and caring about others, whereas men thought in terms of rights. Personal relationships seemed to be more important to women. From birth they showed a keener interest than males in human faces. The male and female brain have been discovered to develop at different rates, equipping girls with verbal and social skills at an earlier age. Over the centuries women have developed skills through natural selection. In early societies domestic work and child-rearing were reasonably handed over to the mothers; now domestic and child-rearing skills are genetic. Or perhaps the needs of the children bring about sexual division of labour. The baby creates the nurturing mother who is tender, but since a tender person cannot protect the infant in the wild, the father becomes hunter and fighter. These are the conclusions of women professionally studying women. They are the arguments of the 1980s, and they are not to be dismissed lightly.

Where do they leave us? There is no going back, no prodigal's return to the kitchen, no fond farewell to the outside world. Yet how can we go forward in a working world created for man, but with a mother's responsibility? Well, there are ways. Women are proving it by doing it. This book takes a look at such women.

1
What do Women Want?

One of the most important changes in the past fifteen years has been the increase in the number of women who achieve professional success and who, at the same time, mother children. The increase has been remarkable, but the number is still small. These women remain exceptions. Yet these exceptional women exhibit a new pattern, a new image which has cracked the established stereotype. We now have a different sense of what women can be, and of what they want to be.

The new image is strong enough to shatter the old, but it still contains some confused, often contradictory, aspects. It emerged with the promise to solve all women's problems; it rose high on the expectation that these problems would be solved. And because these expectations have not been met, the new image, before it could be fully tested and tried, is in danger of subsiding. Already there is a resurgence of the romantic notion of motherhood as female destiny and therefore as fulfilment. As in all extreme positions a backlash

1

is inevitable. The rediscovery of the value of traditional women's roles may drown the more subtle and confused truths within the first unrealistic hopes.

Women's problem has always been that they understood how important mothering was to them. They knew the range of its pleasures – from the sensuousness of the infant's skin to the pride of discovering that a separate individual has emerged from one's care. Women have been held back because they are susceptible to these pleasures and to the value of nurturing small people. Certainly social disapproval, limited opportunity, biased education, have played their part in tying women to the home. But the 'conspiracy against women' has not, for the past fifty years, been so strong as to impede a truly determined woman. The real impediment has come from the mother knot – from her bond to her children, from the necessity of putting her children first. A woman knows, from the beginning, that she will respond helplessly to her children's needs. Selfishness will fail to function as she becomes locked into the well-being of her family.

In some societies mothers can work alongside their children. We can think of Chinese peasants working in the fields with infants on their backs and toddlers rollicking beside them. We can think of the Indian woman pausing in her tasks to nurse her child. But in our society the only way we could possibly work alongside our children is to have them cared for in a nearby creche. This is policy in those countries which value women's work – such as China and Russia and many of the Scandinavian countries. But in Britain and America, where jobs are scarce, unemployment among women is encouraged as a way to ease the problem of unemployment. Sentimental notions of the family are used by politicians to isolate women – because a woman will be isolated with her children if there is no good alternative care available. Her children come first. Even if she does not think they should come first, she will feel and respond as though they do.

The mother knot creates difficulties for the woman. As much as she needs to see the well-being of her children secured, she also needs to satisfy herself. It was once a convenient theory that the needs of the mother and the woman were pretty much one – especially if you added love for a husband as well. What more could a woman want? What was wrong with her, that she seemed to want something else? Other needs were unimaginable. They made no sense. The women's movement shocked people by declaring she wanted what men had – the power to achieve financial independence, the self-esteem which comes from highly regarded work, and the opportunity to engage in work which provides challenge, expansion of skills, and recognition and reward for one's abilities. These needs, and the personality which emerged in an attempt to meet these needs, has been labelled 'expansive' by prominent women psychoanalysts.[1] It is in sharp distinction to dependency needs and a dependent personality, which women have been encouraged to develop, partly in compensation for their unfulfilled expansive needs and partly in response to the nurturing needs of their children.

All people have difficulty combining these two types of needs – particularly in our society, where different values at home and in the workplace heighten the different characteristics and qualities and procedures needed to satisfy these two types of needs. All people make compromises, accept trade-offs, as they juggle these needs. Psychology is rich with studies of such conflicts and of their failed solutions. The type of conflict which is of particular interest in this book, however, is a new conflict arising specifically in women who are acknowledging their expansive needs but who have not learned how to accommodate, or admit, their remaining dependency needs.

Women had a long way to go, but it was not easy to be patient, not when something was so drastically wrong. Ten years ago women were seen as less than fully human. A devastating and unintentionally witty study was conducted in 1970 which revealed a general prejudice. A list of personality traits was sent to three different groups of psychotherapists, with three different sets of instructions. One group was asked to indicate which traits on the list would be found in a 'mature, healthy, socially competent male'. A second group was asked to indicate which personality traits would be found in a 'mature, healthy, socially competent woman'. The third group was asked to consider what traits would describe the 'mature, healthy, socially competent adult'. The first group, which consisted of both men and women, indicated that the mature healthy male would be dominant, aggressive, able to control his feelings and to distinguish thought from emotion. The second group, which also consisted of men and women, were unanimous in their descriptions of the mature healthy female as dependent, home-oriented, susceptible to influence, quick to express emotion, and ready to endorse the emotional rather than the logical side of an argument. So the men and women who professionally dealt with helping people to solve problems of adjustment and compromise accepted the gender stereotypes. This was disappointing, to say the least, but the real punch in the study came from the fact that the group which described the mature healthy adult indicated the same qualities used to describe the mature healthy man.[2] The mature healthy woman, therefore, was not considered to be a mature adult, but something quite different – something immature, perhaps, or even pathological.

This study was done when the women's movement was at full strength. Here was a popular movement telling women to be firm, to be fierce, to be independent and even selfish, to turn their backs on the men to whom they were used to looking for support – a movement which opened up such truths that it seemed to release many women from a prison. Yet because the women who embraced the tenets of feminism had grown up amid the stereotype of a dependent, compliant woman, they experienced considerable anxiety when faced with the realisation of feminist goals.

This anxiety was exhibited first of all by women's antagonism towards the success of other women. Should they not be pleased to see another woman break through prejudice, discard traditional patterns and expectations? Was not that precisely what they had been fighting for? Yes, but we are not always ready to welcome the spoils of victory, es-

pecially when the battle is waged against self-limitation, because those limits, however unfair, have grown comfortable,
and their removal creates anxiety. *Ms* magazine acknowledged this problem in 1976 with an article 'Trashing, The
Dark Side of Sisterhood'. Achievement or accomplishment
of any kind, it was said, was seen to be a crime. 'If you are
assertive – if you do not fit the conventional stereotype of a
feminine woman it's all over . . . The values of the Movement favor women who are self-effacing . . . Women exhibiting potential for achievement are punished by both women
and men.' In response the readership admitted they shared
this disillusion. They agreed that the more success a woman
had, the greater the hostility she aroused in other women.
'Behind every successful woman', one reader wrote, 'is
another woman ready to stab her in the back.'

Were women hopeless bitches – or was there some other
explanation, and some way out of this contradiction? The
hostility directed towards successful women stemmed from
envy and anxiety. It was the hostility of the self-effacing,
compliant, dependent personality towards those who were
able to consider themselves first, have confidence in themselves, and act for themselves. Women had seen such characteristics in men, and had disguised their envy with
admiration, choosing men who could fulfil for them their
unacknowledged desires. But here were women, just like
them, who were experiencing success at first hand. These
successful women reminded others of their own failure.
They proved that their sacrifices were not part of an inevitable destiny. They stimulated their own expansive needs,
but these, when they came up against their dependency
needs, created profound turmoil. The dependent woman
saw self-assertion as aggression, and made a counterattack.

Nor did the successful women have much tolerance for
the typical dependent woman. The typical woman, with her
commitments and attachment to others, represented potential self-defeat. Thus men were strongly attacked – not only
because they were seen to hold the strings of power, but
because they might arouse in women affection, protective-
ness, a desire for children who would in turn arouse

5

affection and the demand to be nurtured. Men had to be attacked because they might tip the balance of a woman's needs. They were the enemy because the enemy was within, and therefore the enemy was everywhere. Above all one wanted to avoid men as potential fathers. Indeed, the women's movement virtually ignored motherhood, because the prospect of pitting oneself against one's children was too awful. Women knew they would never have wives to look after their children, or to look after them, and so when they learnt to value their expansive needs, they ignored their dependency needs.

The new woman tried to act and think like a man. But somehow, as she did so, she did not function as well as a man functions. Perhaps he had had more training than she in self-assertion. While all people have trouble with this, and with aggression, men have usually been encouraged to deal with it since childhood, and many women come to it for the first time as adults. They may be unused to the language of self-assertion or aggression, and respond with the language of dependency – they may burst into tears when criticised, or try to gain influence in their work by being seductive. Such tactics sometimes work, but more often they hold a woman back, and make her colleagues uncomfortable or they offer proof that she is not to be taken seriously. But this difficulty is superficial, and can be overcome with a little self-awareness and discipline.

Far more distressing is the deep-rooted split within herself between her career ambitions and her dependency needs. It does seem that it is more difficult for women to see themselves as separate people, or to consider their needs first and to ignore the feelings of others.[3] This may stem not from the influence of crude stereotypes but from more subtle psychological development in childhood. Mothers and daughters remain more closely connected than do parents and sons. Daughters grow up with a clear idea of themselves in relation to others, and when they are adults they are expected to transfer this relational identity to their husband and children. When they do this they are following the traditional female pattern, but when they engage in identity work – that is, when they seek their identity in terms of work and feel they need to work, and to succeed in their work in order to have a meaningful identity – they are following what was once a predominantly male pattern, one which may create gross conflicts because the first pattern, though consciously discarded, still functions strongly in their lives.

It is in the conflict between the need to fulfil oneself through work and a woman's susceptibility to others' needs and to her own need for others, that new psychological problems have arisen. The various problems of this type have been documented by a leading American psychoanalyst, Dr Alexandra Symonds.[4] She found that many women were seeking her help because she was a female analyst, and they believed that only a woman could understand their problems. These problems were found in apparently liberated women who pursued careers previously considered male, such as law, medicine, business, television management, photography and psychotherapy. They were women who knew that women's lives had to change, and that the new opportunities would improve their chances of fulfilment. They embraced the new maturity, which eschewed sexual stereotypes. But the new life had not brought them happiness. At one extreme Symonds found women whose dependency needs were so deeply denied and repressed that they were not accommodated to any extent. These women avoid affection and intimacy and become controlling and exploitative people. They mimic the man who embraces the macho image and are stunted by affectionatelessness. The point of every encounter is to prove oneself, and one therefore cannot give anything of oneself. This small group of 'liberated' women will not be discussed in this book because they do not become mothers. Yet they do frequently appeal to a wide range of women. Was this not the ideal presented by Colette Dowling in *The Cinderella Complex* – a woman who never relied upon anyone, who would always pursue her own interests first, who hardened herself to any weakness and to need? It was a shallow, distorted ideal, and yet it was vastly popular because it seemed to solve the problems

7

women face today. But of course it would solve nothing; it would only bury and further confuse the conflict.

At the other extreme of women with conflicts between dependency and expansiveness, Symonds found successful career women who have deep, intense and indeed insatiable needs to be taken care of underlying a thin facade of self-sufficiency. Their development appears paradoxical, for they expend a tremendous amount of energy on their education and careers, but they feel that without a man, and without children, they have no true status. These women believe that self identity can only be found in challenging and rewarding work, but they feel they are worthless if they do not have the traditional female supports. Often such women have inherited from their parents (usually their mothers) a low esteem of women. Perhaps, since they are achievement oriented, they were given a double message from their mothers – the common advice from a dissatisfied woman to her daughter: 'Don't be like me.' The mother thereby expresses resentment of her lot, and pushes her daughter to be different; this seems to be a positive influence, but it runs up against two snags. The first is that the daughter does identify with her mother anyway, and a mother's self-dissatisfaction will be passed on to her daughter. Why should she think well of herself if her mother is to be disparaged? Secondly, the mother who gives such negative advice is resentful, and she is likely to resent any success her daughter actually achieves. This will either inhibit the daughter's further success, or will make her highly anxious about her achievements. Also, the mother may – often indirectly – taunt the girl about her lack of traditional female fulfilment. She may remark that if she had not put so much into her career she would have a family by now, or she may emphasise the danger of putting off having children for too long, or suddenly wax eloquent about the joys of motherhood. The mother feels threatened by the daughter's success because it is a sign of independence, and since she is dissatisfied with her own life, she cannot accept the loss of her daughter. It is better to keep her daughter down than to lose her. The daughter in turn ceases to find any value in the fruits of her efforts and needs to prove herself along more traditional lines. She inherits her mother's low self-esteem and needs a man to be of importance on her behalf.

Between the extremes of women who totally deny dependency needs and those who feel they are nothing without a man, is the largest group of career women. These women have achieved success in their working lives and some satisfaction in their personal lives, but they none the less feel dissatisfied, and believe that their dissatisfaction comes from not succeeding enough either at home or at work, and so they try doubly hard at each. Many studies of women and men in the professions show that women tend to have more children than their male peers, and that they have more children because they want to prove their femininity but at the same time they want to pursue the careers that are so important to them.[5] These women hope to prove that they are sacrificing nothing and cheating no one either at home or at work. They give a great deal to everyone – sometimes compulsively – because they want to feel that they do their best, because they want to prove that no one will suffer from their double life. After all, they have chosen it, and it is up to them to prove that it is possible.

These women exhibit the superwoman syndrome, which is fuelled primarily by guilt. The woman feels her dual responsibilities – she does not accept a change in her responsibilities at home, and she hankers after further responsibility at work. She takes pride in self-sufficiency, but self-sufficiency takes its toll. She is keen to nurture others, but is slow to accept being nurtured. She gives her husband and children support but feels that they should not make allowances for her or be limited by her needs because she has already inconvenienced them enough by working, and by being committed to her career. These women have chosen identity work, but they also have chosen to have a family, and they want to protect their families from the implications of that choice. They cannot accept functioning in what seems to them a selfish manner – though it may well be the typical male manner – and they worry continuously about what their work habits are doing to their families.

They cannot accept support from their husbands or boy-friends in the way that they offer support to men because they believe they do not deserve it, because they do not know how to accept it. Women do not know how to make wives of men. They are used to giving, not receiving support. They encourage people to depend upon them and to make demands upon them because they appear so competent, energetic and self-sufficient. As a result they suffer undue stress, fatigue and depression, yet they remain ashamed of their dependency needs, and suffer in silence.

In spite of the emotional wear and tear most women do not give up either on their careers or their families. And how could a woman give up on one or the other? Her work is essential to her, yet she is keenly responsive to her family's needs – and the needs of her children are seldom as short-lived as she might have planned. 'As soon as they are at school . . .' is a hopeful but seldom fulfilled refrain, as mothers of adolescents discover. But if she becomes a super-woman she need give up nothing. It is a simple, if crude solution. The trouble is that it is not a solution. Women have to seek new ways to balance their needs. They must discover the true balance of their needs. This book looks at the working mother's problems in general and at some out-standing solutions. It is a book about exceptional women, who may in fact represent what all women need.

2
Why do Women Mother?

Is Motherhood an Invention?

'Mothering' means something different from 'fathering'. To father is to be a biological parent. To mother is to bear a child, but also to nurture it, care for it, love it as a particular sort of parent. Motherhood was given short shrift by the feminists of the 1970s. It was expected that motherhood would change beyond all recognition. More and more women would choose not to have children. Mothering would become a job chosen by a few women, who would look after all the children born to a society. These suggestions seem ridiculous now. Reformists always tend to over-estimate the rate of change. If motherhood changes, it will take a long time to change drastically. Children have half a mother's genes, and, biosocially, one can expect that she will be interested in caring for her children until they

11

survive as independent adults. And then the child, too, is adept at manipulating the mother. In all societies the child exhibits especially appealing behaviour, eliciting in the mother very strong attachment responses.

It has been suggested, however, that motherhood is invented, that the close bond between child and mother is unnatural, that it has been forced upon her by the nuclear family, which is an aberration from the normal extended family. Well, the notion of the extended family is a myth. In Britain and America the family has been nuclear since the middle ages.[1] The main change in motherhood in Britain in the middle decades of this century was the decline of the nanny who had taken over the daily chores of child care along with the issues of discipline, eating, toilet training – which are now so carefully guarded by the parents. A mother's visits to the nursery have sometimes been described as state occasions, whereby an important, idealised and loved woman comes to spend a few moments with her child. Such distance is not unheard of now, though it is no longer part of an institution. But it was never common, and was always linked to what was thought best for the child. Earlier practices, too, of farming out children to wet nurses arose from beliefs about what was best for the child. There was, after all, no alternative to natural feeding, and it was often thought that the mother's own milk was not good for the child – should she become pregnant while feeding, the nourishment would go to the embryo and the existing infant would starve. Sex would curdle the milk, but sex and pregnancy were not easily avoided. The practices which seemed to distance the child from the mother were endorsed on behalf of the child and were not a sign of coolness or indifference.

The most positive and telling point about motherhood to emerge from the women's movement is that children have two parents. Why should all the care fall to the mother? Why should her life be dominated by the children, while the father, who had equal reasons, in biosocial terms – the child had half his genes, too – for caring for the child, left it all to the mother? The answer was in terms of male exploitation. Looking after children was a boring task, mindless, with few rewards. Therefore men, because they had the power to do so, left it to women.

The feminists of the last decade were right to insist there was no obvious logic in the assumption that women mother. Motherhood is, among other things, a social institution. Ready-made patterns make it easy for the female parent to mother, and difficult for her not to mother. She has, in terms of general acceptance, permission to stay at home, not to work outside the home, whereas the father does not. Choices and desires emerge among possibilities, and it is easier for a woman to recognise and acknowledge her desire to care for the children than it is for a man. If the social set-up were different, would not more men recognise their capacities of nurturing children?

Females bear children and have the capacity to nurse them, but from these facts it is not at all clear that long-term mothering is inevitable, or natural or the best possible arrangement. Some psychoanalysts have postulated mothering instincts, or a need or drive to mother which follows pregnancy, and believe that pregnancy is accompanied by psychological and emotional preparation to mother. A more elaborate and bizarre and manipulative theory is that holding the baby in her uterus leads the woman to identify with it after birth and gives her a 'very powerful sense of what the baby needs'.[2] Theories like this, whatever truth they may contain, are misleading because they suggest a closed system between biological input and behaviour or feeling, which would suggest that there was no room for variation, or that variations in behaviour and attitude and feelings indicate not healthy choices, not adaptability to one's needs or one's family's needs, b abnormality. Women's maternal responses, howeve vary. Some are immediately responsive to their inf seduced away from previous interests and ne women do not feel fully bound to their childr are a little older. And some women are willi that intense maternal bonding to the mothers. This is not common, but it i

13

Can Fathers 'Mother'? – Role Reversal

Cases of role reversal, where the father becomes the prime psychological parent, are increasing. They are still rare – too rare to prove anything about parents in general – but they do show that it is possible for the father to choose to be the main caretaker, not in the way that a traditional father who loses his wife remains just like a father, though he is in fact the only parent, but that it is possible for the couple to choose to give the bulk of daily care, the continued, immediate presence and attention, which we call nurturing, to the father.

This is a topic of current interest. If fathers can easily assume the role of mother, then would that not prove that it is simply the common set-up which forces women into the maternal role? Would it not prove that fathers are as adept as women at mothering, if we only gave them a chance? And women would then be as free as men to pursue their other interests – or would they?

As a child I remember reading a story about a man who slighted women's work and claimed that his wife had an easy time of things while he went out to do hard work all day. His wife then challenged him to trade jobs for one day. The woman succeeded brilliantly, for she already knew his work on the farm, but the husband had no idea how to proceed with her work and by the end of the day was humiliated. Role reversal is still sometimes seen in this comic and superficial light. Last year a movie was released in the US called *Mr Mom*, in which a husband is made redundant, and the wife is able to find a lucrative job. He takes over the domestic chores, runs into innumerable practical difficulties and reveals remarkable stupidity (he tries to dry a child's hair with a hoover). The film pretends to play up the idea that women are superior, better able to cope, more efficient, but in fact takes the well-worn, inconsequential line that I had found in my childhood reader. *Kramer vs Kramer* was a far more sophisticated attempt at the study of role reversal. In the film the father develops the primary caretaker's attachment to his son while suffering the frustrations and set-backs and juggled priorities a working mother would face. The film was in that sense an improvement upon the novel on which it was based. Avery Corman's novel reads like a fairy tale of paternal fulfilment: the father found a dream housekeeper, sensible, reliable, loving, who took care of the daily nitty-gritty, while he discovered that the new depth of his attachment to his son actually enhanced his capacity to work, injecting new life into his ideas and energies. In the film, the mother, freed from her child, becomes more successful than her husband at work and, after winning back custody of the child in court, lets the father keep the son because she acknowledges the bond that has formed between them. In the novel the mother's meanness in abandoning the child is highlighted by its pointlessness. She manages to get a job as a secretary in a tennis club, but shows no promise for self-fulfilment or success. Her aversion to motherhood was for the chores, the endless demands, the tedious obligations. In the film, however, the mother's dilemma is put concisely and tragically in the first few minutes. 'I'm no good for him or for myself', she says. She loses her temper a hundred times a day. She loves her son but her own frustration renders that love useless. She cannot control her irritation, and despairs at the effect of her temper upon her son. Every full-time mother knows what this is like.

These two films, for all their faults, show the two general reasons for role reversal. The father takes on the role of mother either because the woman has a higher paying job than the father, or because the father has to become mother, when the mother leaves the family for some reason. She may have abandoned the family, and therefore her absence will be accompanied by anger and bewilderment. Or the mother may die, and however great a part anger and bewilderment play in grief, they are tempered by a retrospective and intensified love, and an ability, eventually, to incorporate the dead person into oneself. It is not an easier situation when someone dies, it is not an emotionally happier situation, but it is in some sense simpler, and it does seem to leave roles untouched. The father may become more involved in his children when the mother dies, but he does not take on the role of mother, as he sometimes does when she leaves. But when he does this, it is as a working parent, not as a full-time mothering parent.

Yet the first example of role reversal I witnessed was immensely promising in that it showed a father gradually taking primary responsibility for his children, as he discovered that he was more responsive to them than their mother. The renowned economist Joseph Stiglitz found himself to be the prime parent of his three-year-old son and five-year-old daughter even before his wife decided to leave him. His wife was suffering a typical and tragic split in her needs. She was ambitious, too, as an economist, and she knew she was an able economist, but the distraction of two young children made the concentration and self-development necessary to her career impossible. Joe Stiglitz was always a loving parent, but he shrewdly weighed up the work children required, and he was glad to allocate it to someone else. The Stiglitz family always employed au pairs or nannies, with the inevitable ups and downs in benefits. Some of the young women employed to look after their children were excellent at their jobs, but created time cost themselves, if they were ill or distressed. Some of them talked too much, leaving them with no private time, and some of them left without giving satisfactory notice. But they did always have someone with whom they could legitimately leave the children. Stiglitz's first wife took more and more advantage of this arrangement, until she was spending no more than four hours a week with the children who, in turn, became more demanding, more irritating, when she was with them. Her distraction was aggravated by a serious love affair which could also be understood in terms of her need for self-confirmation, or for a confirmation of a self beyond that of mother. When the marriage was clearly at an end, but they were still hanging on, as many couples do, bewildered as to how, in practical terms, to end the marriage, Joe suggested that he take the children. For his wife this was a solution, and she accepted with alacrity – not easily, not without heartbreak, but readily, because she knew this had to be the solution. She could not be a full-time mother. So Joe became a **Mr Kramer**, and quickly weighed up the 'utility' – as he called it in an economist's terms. He did not want to look after his children alone. It was difficult, it was tiring, it was often boring and, what was most important, it reduced his 'output' – that is, the number of papers he could write and articles he could prepare for publication. But he would prefer these losses to losing daily contact with his children. It was naturally more than he had bargained for – single parenting is always more than anyone has bargained for. His five-year-old daughter would become hysterical if the nanny took her to school when she had thought her father would. Joe spent five days at a conference in Mexico, and returned to find the girl virtually a nervous wreck. He was surprised by the extent of his children's needs, but he accepted the new bond. He tempered his anxiety with humour. Optimism served him well, so that he was able to look upon this crisis state as temporary. What were clearly absent, and what would in all probability have plagued a mother in a similar position, were fear of financial doom and, above all, guilt. Most women would fear for their financial future, but he of course had his earning power. His current assets were halved upon his divorce, but he never feared poverty. Most important, however, he saw himself as an innocent victim. He had done the normal thing, had had the usual expectations of a wife, but though he had not done anything 'wrong', everything had gone wrong around him. He did not take the blame upon himself, and he did not take upon himself the blame for his children's distress. It was not that he cast all the blame upon his wife. He was naturally angry with her, and bewildered by her apparent neglect of the children, but he did not throw stones at her and whitewash himself. He simply saw no point in blame or guilt, no point in wondering whether he should have tried harder for the children's sake, or wondering what crucial mistakes he had unwittingly made. A clear conscience made it much easier for him to cope with problems as they arose – not to second guess his children's needs, not to despair when he had exceeded his luck and indulged in too much freedom, but to learn from his mistakes and gradually to test the ground for recovery. A woman, as a mother, tends to take the blame for all injury – both physical and mental – to her children. Thus she is so distressed by her own short temper, by her own inattention, by her own ambitions, she may conclude that her children are better off without her. Joe became the prime parent, and accepted primary responsibility for the children, without that peculiar psychological responsibility many women take, a responsibility for the well-being of their children which goes beyond reason, beyond sense, and which stems not simply from training or stereotyped expectations of mother love, but from the truth behind those myths – the truth that the mother identifies her self with her children in the way a man does not.

But the father is usually sufficiently attached to his children to become the primary parent in the mother's absence. The father's attachment is real and strong, but it does not usually develop in the same naked way. Motherhood is an institution whereby the mother is isolated with her child. Not only is she left at home with the child, but any outing with the child is often difficult. And when a mother breaks this bond to her home and to her children, when she 'leaves home' as fathers do, she usually effects some kind of permanent break. Even though she may see her children, she does so half-heartedly, because in leaving them at all she has killed something in herself. This happens to many men, too, fathers who have left the family and who grow more and more distant; but though this does happen, many fathers I spoke to, fathers who were divorced from their children's mothers, made a special effort to minimise the separation from their children. 'When we were married', explains a working mother of a seven-year-old boy, 'his work was sacred. But now that we're divorced he has to make time for his son. He's never before spent so much time with him.' The father explained. 'When we were married I felt that my wife was caring for Daniel for me. But now we're apart I feel I have to impress upon him my individuality. I have to establish a relationship with him myself, because he's bound to see us as separate people, now that we're living apart. When we were married I could just be there and feel there was some connection. But now if I'm going to have any link with him I have to spend time with him myself.'

As in any individual story there are elements which put everything in a highly specific setting and make one wonder whether any generalisations can be drawn from it at all. This father, who is a highly articulate Oxford don, felt that he dissolved his marriage partly because his identification with his son was so strong that he could not respond sexually to his son's mother. For him his wife had become mother only, and he could not live with her as man and wife. He separated himself from the family because he was engulfed by it. He was a child, was the same as the child in that domestic setting, and to be a father he had to leave. But fathers leave the family for many reasons, and some are not able to reestablish a more independent bond with their children. On the other hand, no woman is likely to do so. Her attachment is so intense that something withers when she separates herself from her children, in the intense mothering years. She may see them, but they become dead to her. She may – indeed she undoubtedly will – suffer greatly from her memory of maternal feelings, but they will no longer be functional. They will be like pains in amputated limbs.

The Short Life-expectancy of Role Reversal

When Joe Stiglitz found himself to be the primary parent he retained, under great pressure, an ebullience and optimism that no woman could sustain. He had after all the confidence in his work, the supremacy of professional concentration that is common to a professional man. Women may share it, and more and more women are coming to share it, but it is won with self-conscious effort, still, and maintained under seige of expectations that the career will lose its priority when children make particularly strong demands. Often these threats come from within – imagined voices from childhood, or remembered expectations – but they are none the less real and forceful influences and we have reason to fear them. When a professional man becomes a single parent, his work may be under stress, but not under seige. He may be impossibly busy, and he may even cut down for a while – but he accepts this on a temporary basis. Neighbours, friends, and certainly a girlfriend or wife will take over the bulk of the parent's duties. The children will be very good at involving the girlfriend in their care, even if she should be atypically slow in finding her role. And why should he not view his position as temporary? All children have two parents, and all children may need two parents, but also all parents need to share the children. We may learn how to survive as single parents, but very few people thrive as single parents, and most people who are surviving as single parents are looking hard and fast for a relief parent. A man who becomes the primary parent and who manages that role is doing a temporary job. As with all temporary jobs it may become permanent, but he is justified in his optimism. People will help his him with the house and with the children in a way they will not help a single mother because she, after all, is used to her job.

Sometimes role reversal is deliberate. A couple will decide that the father will stay at home to take on the jobs traditionally allocated to the mother, and that the woman will go out to work, thereby supporting the family. This decision is almost always made on a financial basis – the woman has a higher paying job than the husband – but the range of considerations is wider than financial ones because it is often a costly set-up in other ways. It is difficult, very difficult, for a woman to give up her privileged position as mother. The physical bond, though not necessarily overriding, though not unanswerable to other interests, is none the less present, and the child that is hers in one sense – the natural sense of having given birth to it – may seem hers by rights in other areas too. Some mothers are better at sharing their children than others. Many women manoeuvre their husbands out of child-rearing because they want exclusive rights over them, and then complain because they are left with the bulk of the responsibility.

Women have not had good lessons in sharing their children, just as they have not had good lessons in refraining from accepting blame for everything that goes wrong with their children. Their possessiveness embraces the burdens that have been thrust upon them. To give up sole possession means relinquishing one sure point of identity, and accepting primary domestic possession means, for the man, threatening a commonplace identity. But of the five couples I spoke to who had decided upon role reversal, there was not one for whom it did not work – temporarily.

One woman feared that she would be jealous of her husband when she returned to work, but found that she was not. Another woman said she loved her child, but felt no urge to mother him in the usual way. She felt her husband would be more patient than she would be, and that he would enjoy it more. Another woman, Sara, who works as an editor with the *New Yorker* magazine, felt that she could only have turned over the care of their child to the father, not to a housekeeper. Her husband, Emil, taught law at New York University Law School, but was not promoted at the usual time. He worried that his contract would be terminated and that it would be difficult to find another job. When their son was born they decided that Sara's career was more assured. Even if she did not stay with the *New Yorker* she would find other jobs or get other work. (If Emil gave up his teaching job he might have time to prepare work for publication and thereby increase his chances for future employment.) It was not a clear-cut decision here as it was in most other cases of deliberate role reversal. Usually the woman had a secure position and the man was relinquishing a dull or low-paid job. As in any case where the path is not absolutely clear, anxiety about having made the right choice can make any choice more difficult. At first they suffered tremendous tension, though they now say that part of it was simply the change a baby brought to their lives. They had been an independent New York working couple, and now their life-style was transformed. Emil found it difficult to work at home, and Sara hated leaving the child, though she thought part of her dread stemmed from guilt inflicted by Emil's unhappiness. The initial stress subsided, but Sara found that she wanted to interfere at every point. She wanted to decide when the baby needed to see a doctor, how the child should be disciplined, what kind of things the child should eat. At work she worried obsessively about accidents. Every time the phone rang she imagined that Emil was going to tell her their son's eye had been poked out, or that he had been burned, or dropped, or kidnapped while walking in the park. Such fears are normal, but they were exaggerated in Sara's case because they were linked to her guilt about not mothering the child: her ambivalence towards the child was peculiarly threatening because her positive feelings were not reinforced by the hundred swings of feeling that confront a caretaker during the course of the day. She came home in the evening to witness a unit that seemed complete without her. The son became primarily attached to the father, would turn to him when distressed, would be jealous of his, not the mother's, interest in others, would ask him first for food, for a toy, for a story. Therefore Sara had to accept what a working mother who has a working husband does not have to accept – the child's attitude of primary trust and dependence upon the father. In all the dual-career families I saw or spoke to, the children still looked upon the mother with decided preference, still came to the mother when hurt or unhappy. Only when the roles were decidedly reversed, not shared, did the child focus primarily upon the father.

Both Sara and Emil believed they were better off without full-time paid child care. Though they were well off, a full-time housekeeper in New York costs about $12 000 plus medical insurance payments, and is not, contrary to what I have often heard said, tax deductible. That is, only $200 per child is deductible for child care, and that does not go very far. If it is to be deducted, then the husband and wife must file together for income tax consideration, and that is not always reasonable for a two-income family. Also, Sara believed she could not trust anyone other than herself or her husband with her child. She knew that reliable nannies or housekeepers existed, but she did not trust her luck to find one, and she trusted her husband because he alone shared with her the passionate concern for the child's well-being. If she was going to be out all day, and would sometimes have to be away for a few days at a time, she wanted to be sure her child was with someone who loved him. 'I felt like a male chauvinist pig', she admitted, 'but for the first time I saw some humanity in the husband's desire for the wife to be home.' Her wish for the husband to look after the child, if she could not, was not a power struggle, a desire to keep the husband in a secure and limited place, but a recognition that her husband would express love on her behalf. He alone could 'parent' the child if she was at work all day. Her husband, initially, was glad to do this. He was proud to be able to look after his child, and to get to know his needs. Clashes between mother and father occurred primarily when Sara seemed to doubt Emil's ability to handle and understand the child. Once, when the boy was being particularly objectionable, in the way children frequently are, and Sara had had a tiring day at work, she blamed Emil for letting the child get overtired, whereas Emil said the boy could not sleep because he was feeling unwell. Sara said she eventually learnt to trust Emil's judgement, though this was at first a blow to her pride. She believed she should know the boy's needs best – as indeed she did at the end of three months' maternity leave, but not after Emil had been looking after him for six months. Emil felt special in this regard, for though it is more common now that men share child care, rarely do they take it over, rarely do they become the parent who knows when children need their teeth checked, their next tetanus shot, a new shoe size.

The grandparents of this father-nurtured child had an important influence on his parents' ability to choose and adapt to role reversal. Though Emil's father was away from home during the day, and his mother took the traditional female part in bringing up her children, his father showed affection more openly, more physically than did many other fathers of that generation, and this, he believes, allows him to be demonstrative and expressive without fear. Sara's

mother, on the other hand, gave her permission to relinquish a primary mothering role in a largely negative way.
She was hugely affectionate, but also domineering. She resented her position as a woman, was aware of men's dislike
of women, and countered her subjection with an hostility
that made her, in her daughter's eyes, ugly. Sara suffered
from a matrophobia which was not so much fear of her
mother as fear of being a mother. What would bearing a
child do to her? Would she then face the frustration which
turned her mother into a monster? Would she suffer the
rage against men and against her own child which she had
seen in her own mother? Sara had put off having children
for several years, fearing these things, but when she was
thirty she felt she had to have one now, or not all. The
couple's decision that Emil would 'mother' the child made
it easier for her.

Like all the cases of role reversal I witnessed, this one
was successful, but like the rest, it was temporary. After
looking after their son full time for eighteen months, Emil
found Daniel a nursery – with difficulty, as New York is
not teeming with suitable nursery facilities. Daniel was to
attend it from eight-thirty – Sara would drop him off on
her way to work – until three, when Emil would collect
him. This suited Sara, for she believed that the nursery and its
staff would be better able to avoid the accidents she dreaded
in her own home, with someone less watchful, or less inti-
mately concerned than a parent. Emil had been pleased with
his job as parent, but he was also failing to complete any work
projects. He had done more than most fathers, he said.

He had indeed done more than most fathers, and he was
justified in his pride, and justified in his self-defence. The
fact that he had not done nearly as much as most mothers
should not be held against him. All the role-reversal fathers
knew that their time at home, full time, would be limited.
They would go back to work as soon as they reasonably
could. None of them envisaged staying at home until the
children were teenagers. In fact, none of them envisaged
staying at home to look after two children. All the couples
who practised role reversal by choice were strictly one-child

families. The men who mothered knew that their full-time jobs would not be long in demand, and they helped to accelerate the process from full-time to part-time parenting. When Daniel was two and a half, his father got another job, and Sara elected to work part time, and to have another child. She had overcome her matrophobia, and developed a fear of missing out as a mother. Whereas her husband showed foresight in seeing the intense stage of parenting as temporary, she was quicker than most men to understand the brevity of childhood as an opportunity not to be missed.

High-earning Mothers and Male Parents

Role reversal never simply changed the male parent into a mother. The father brought his knowledge of the needs for work into play, and the mother was reluctant to forego the special privileges of motherhood. It was rare, too, and I did not find any cases of role reversal among highly successful women, or highly ambitious women, where it would have been more feasible. The husband, then, would not have had a financial reason for returning to work so soon, and he could have had a housekeeper to help him. I asked one lawyer, the mother of three children, who was earning a staggering $250 000 a year, why her husband did not consider staying at home. She had picked up Jane O'Reilly's witty point that a wife would be a wonderful thing to have – someone to look after your social life, your clothes, your home, your children, someone whose job it was to relieve you of the burden not only of doing domestic tasks but also of organising someone to get them done, even of thinking about them or knowing of their existence. Why didn't her husband, whose reasonable salary as an elected judge was insignificant compared to hers, become her wife? 'Because I wouldn't like him to', she admitted. 'I'd feel awful coming home to someone who had been at home all day. And I know I'd have less freedom if he stayed home because I could not justify doing as much as I do if he weren't having a good time too – I mean a good time in his work, stretching himself as much as he wants.'

There were obvious reasons why role reversal among highly successful women was, as far as I could discover, nonexistent. Whereas ambitious men may be attracted to complacent women, ambitious women are rarely attracted to complacent men. Since these women are attracted to like-minded men, it would be difficult for their men to accept a role reversal. The husband would be frustrated and jealous. Moreover, the wife would be quicker than a conventional man to recognise, accept and even value his dissatisfaction. But most important was the woman's empathy with a homebound person. Even if she had never stayed at home full time, she knew what it would be like. Either her mother had done it and hated it, or had accepted it and cruelly limited herself, or she had seen friends' hopes wither under domestic pressure, or she simply understood her position as someone who had escaped a mould which would have been cruel to her. Whatever the reason, she did not see the possibility of being a traditional wife as a serious one – not for her, and not for anyone she loved. 'Only if I wanted to punish my husband, to teach him a feminist lesson, would I suggest that he stay at home and do nothing but look after the house and the children', this lawyer said. 'I wouldn't do it – how could I ask him to?' Most women, it seems, would not expect a husband to live as they could not happily live. Most working mothers would prefer the pressure of being prime psychological parent to turning their husband into a wife. Perhaps they have a better idea than a man of what it is like to be a wife – or are they naturally more careful in what they ask of other people?

The Feminist Mystique

More and more women are joining the workforce. Fewer women see marriage as an end to their jobs. Children today less frequently have their mothers at home full time. The changing outlook of women upon their working lives, their careers, is the most significant social change of the last decade. At the same time, studies of what women need, what capacities and skills come most naturally to them, how they solve moral dilemmas and what priorities lead to happiness or even merely to mental health, are revealing startling, conservative results.

At the height of the women's movement, feminists tried to spot female traits and responses, and to oust them like toxic influences. Dependency on others, especially on males, was learned – as were weakness, helplessness, uncertainty. Even motherhood was seen as an invention, enforced by patriarchal psychologists and psychoanalysts who claimed either that the mother needed the child for any sense of fulfilment, or that the child needed the mother so desperately that any separation she enforced to fulfil her own selfish needs would maim him or her. Women were kept in a woman's mould by men, who had shaped society to fit their needs, to compensate for their particular failings and fears. Men had also, it was thought, established a society which made it particularly difficult to accommodate a woman in any institution other than that of motherhood, which was in fact man's institution. It did not matter that a woman's dependence on men would destroy her should she be abandoned by a man – it was convenient enough when he wanted it. Motherhood and a mother's outlook made a woman more cautious. Seldom did she have nothing to lose in taking a risk, for her children were involved. Things were probably better for the children as they were, even though she suffered. But man was not woman's only enemy. There was an enemy within, who had been put there by training and by deliberate neglect of a wider vision. Even as women thought they were gaining independence, they were really only biding time until Prince Charming relieved them of responsibility and effort. They were too inclined to be seduced by others' needs, and so were the first to give way at work, the first to hold back in a fight. They had not learned how to be aggressive, and so they continued to be indirect, hoping to persuade others to act for them by sending out coy signals, rather than acting themselves. They were not strong enough to destroy the image they despised.

And so the feminist mystique arose. Women must become like men if they are to succeed as men. They must toss out useless feminine tendencies. They must whip themselves into shape, and not only learn men's games but learn how to play them like a man. Concern for others, when the battle is on, is taboo. They must learn to look out for themselves, to be as ruthless and as dedicated as a man.

The first wave of feminists had either eschewed traditional female roles by refusing to be either wives or mothers, or – and this group formed a decisive majority – they were wives, mothers and liberated women, at least in so far as they pursued careers. There was exhilaration among this group – they no longer had to choose between motherhood and a profession, as had the previous generation. In an American study of women physicians in the Detroit area[3] it was found that today more women were working full time – in fact only 7 per cent of the entire sample were not working for reasons related to being a woman – that is, child-bearing and child-rearing. A higher percentage of women physicians than ever before were board certified (that is, had passed examinations in a medical specialty). Also, more women physicians than in any previous study were seen to have worked continuously full time since graduation. At the same time, these women were having more children – the average number of children was nearly double what it was in 1957 among a similar group – and the number of their children was on average higher than for their male peers. Most of these women (80 per cent) had domestic help at least one day a week, but 76 per cent did all the shopping, cooking, household money management and child care. When these tasks were delegated to domestic help, the women physicians still had the responsibility for household tasks. This is sharply contrasted with the men physicians, almost none of whom either perform household tasks or have responsibility for them – with the exception of money management. These patterns, which were supported by other studies, showed that women who no longer had to choose between family and career, had the responsibility of both. They were keen to prove their femininity and their professionalism. It was the age of the superwoman, who ate her cake, but had to bake it, too.

After all, if child-rearing and home-making were not real jobs – and this is what the liberated woman of the 1970s thought – then she could do it as an aside, while engaged in real work. Men should help, because the tasks could not be wished away, but it often seemed easier for a woman to take on the responsibility herself than to battle endlessly against the husband's domestic indolence. Some women took time to teach their men how to do domestic chores, and some men got into the habit of doing them, but good habits are not as widespread as good theory. If a woman was a superwoman, however, she could be nice as well. She did not have to ask more of anyone – only of herself. This also gave her independence because she was in charge both of her work and of her home. Indeed, many women found that it was no good gaining financial independence if she then had to depend domestically upon someone who let her down. And housekeepers, nurses, nannies, maids and au pairs tend to be far worse than husbands.

Recently women have been having a well-earned laugh at themselves for thinking that they must do everything – that they have a right to be career people only if they have made sure that the home runs smoothly too. But the damnedest thing was that domestic concerns, especially those involved with child-rearing, kept falling into their laps. A woman was so quick to respond to her children's needs, so quick to worry about them and to conclude that she alone could help them when they were ill or unhappy; and her children's desire to have mummy, to do things with her – well that went right to her, and if she managed to extricate herself, she ended up brooding over them for an entire day. Betty Friedan warned against giving way to the feminist mystique, which meant that in embracing liberation, a woman discarded or neglected all those things women were especially good at – such as responsiveness to others and the flexibility that accompanies willingness to accommodate others' needs, and the urge to make a comfortable home and to aid others' happiness.[4] Betty Friedan need not have worried. The feminist mystique is an advertiser's idea, portraying selfishness, drive, ambition, success as glamour. It may also appeal to some young women before they have their own families and discover their own compulsion to care for others; but it is an image which will quickly wear away. Fifteen years after the women's movement began, Colette Dowling appeared to be saying something new when she exhorted women to think like men, to learn to be like men in order to succeed in the workplace.[5] She in fact had said nothing which had not been said many times before – it is just that women were not listening. They tried to listen, but the ideas could not permeate their lives, at least not their lives as mothers.

It was the fault of all that role training, wasn't it? All those dolls we played with, instead of erector sets, all those fairy tales in which a supine (but sometimes devious) beauty was saved by the prince's courage, all that manipulative praise of our looks and our niceness that turned us into good little women.

At first it was exhilarating to see how our training conspired against us, how oppressive were the assumptions that we would give up our own career interests to dedicate ourselves to our families. Women were now given weapons against limiting assumptions and limiting images. They were determined not to pass them on to their children. There were changes, important changes. But the basic fact of the woman being the primary parent – the form and substance of motherhood – that did not change so quickly. Role-training existed, that could not be denied. But role-training does not seem to be the cause of women's persistent mothering. Role-training suggests a model whereby notions are programmed into us, determining our behaviour. It is a crude model, and it does not seem to work, because even when we are careful to avoid such 'programming' we find that women tend to be the primary parent. Motherhood will not budge, not much at any rate.

It is time now to admit that we are stuck. We have gone so far, but not only do we seem unable to go further, we seem to be sliding back, wondering what we worked so hard for, coming to the conclusion that we have traded in motherhood for motherhood and success, and have become exhausted by the trade-offs between them. It is time to take a closer look at why women mother, because the first answers, that once seemed obvious, have lost their meaning.

The Evolution of the Mothering Role

Mothering is not instinctive to women, but it is a strong and persistent tendency. Perhaps women tend to remain the primary parent today because they have been so in the past. They have inherited genes which make them naturally good mothers, which attune them to the needs of others and inculcate in them a need for others. This bioevolutionary argument was presented recently by Alice Rossi, a sociologist who had previously been a staunch feminist spokesperson. She found that sex differences persisted, especially in regard to parenting practices and attitudes, but unlike a good feminist politician, she looked elsewhere than in male conspiracies for an explanation. Sexual division of labour occurred in the earliest societies because it aided survival. Women stayed close to their infants for many reasons. There was no alternative to breast feeding, and so they had to be close to the child. Pregnancy hindered movement, and so for much of the time they would not have made good hunters. Therefore the men hunted, and were separated from the domestic arena, and skills of strength and characteristics like aggression were favoured among them, whereas skills and characteristics appropriate to child-rearing and domesticity were favoured among the women. The division of labour is now biologically built into human sex.[6]

This hypothesis is less of an affront when we look at how it is used. No argument about genes can dictate what we should do. It merely suggests what we might be able to do more easily, and its generalising sweep is a protection against any individual case. For both men and women, attributes and behaviours overlap, and there is a wide range of 'normal'. There may often be greater differences between two normal women, than can be found between a man and a woman. What an hypothesis like Rossi's does is merely to suggest why certain things may come more easily to women than to men. The theory that women are genetically better at mothering does not mean they should mother, or that they should devote themselves to nothing but mothering. But we could use the theory to suggest that if we expect men to become primary parents, or to take a more primary role as parent, then they would require greater training. They would have to be taught what women already know. This approach could make us both more positive and more patient.

There are many other plausible theories about women's genetic suitability to mothering. Her attentiveness to children may have developed from the need to protect the child in primitive societies – women who were not sufficiently attuned to children's needs did not have children who grew to child-bearing age; they were not able to reproduce themselves. This theory is supported by the fact that female infants of three months are much better than male infants of the same age at focusing on and following pictures of faces. Whereas faces catch a female infant's attention, a male infant will not distinguish between a picture of a face and an abstract drawing. This argument, however, seems something of a cheat when put in the context that female infants are quicker at everything. In general, they simply mature more rapidly, so that precosity in one area does not prove anything at all.

The trouble with any genetic theory is that it is at best a convincing story. We cannot trace the development of genes. What is worse, we cannot be sure that mothering has anything to do with genes peculiar to women. There is clearly a lot of untapped parental talent in men – we frequently see the tell-tale tenderness, the empathy and patience – but almost always the specific care for the child falls to the mother. Only if there is a particular reason why this should not be so, is it otherwise. And even if there is some genetic leaning towards this position, there are clearly other reasons too. One cause, closer to home than ancestral hunting societies, and one which every woman experiences, is that she was mothered by a woman. The impulse to nurture one's children, and the desire to have children for whom one cares, is not to be explained in terms of sex differences and sex-linked genes, but in the development of gender.

Sex and Gender

Sex is a biological definition. It refers to the male or female sex and the biological features that detemine whether one is male or female. Gender, on the other hand, designates the areas of behaviour, feelings, thoughts and fantasies that are related to one's sex, yet do not have a specific biological basis. This distinction between sex and gender, which is now widely accepted, was introduced by Dr Robert Stoller[7] who began his studies by trying to find a biological account underlying gender identity and behaviour, but concluded that though there are biological forces which contribute to gender identity, it is primarily culturally determined – or rather, it is determined by the culture as it is funnelled through the mother, and subsequently, through the father, siblings and friends.

This conclusion emerged from Stoller's observations of children whose sex had been misdiagnosed at birth. These extraordinary cases arose when the infant had adrenogenital syndrome. The infant is genetically female, has the hormonal balance of a normal female, and all the internal structures of a normal female, but has an abnormal genital appearance, which makes the genitals appear masculine. If at birth one infant is understood to be female, though exhibiting this syndrome, whereas another is labelled male because of the masculinised genitalia, then the children, at five, have no doubts that they are the sex they were said to be at birth. Each child behaves perfectly normally as a member of the sex she believes herself to be.

Though the new-born's mind is sexually undifferentiated and must be instructed as to its proper sex role, this is taught, and learnt rapidly. In infancy and early childhood it seems that the brain codes notions of masculinity and femininity into coherent and separate systems. Each gender system provides for the child a framework of acceptable and unacceptable behaviour, a framework which depends upon the child's gender identity. Very early the child learns to inhibit behaviour which is not in accord with the appropriate gender. After this framework is learnt, and the behavioural patterns which stem from it are adopted, any behaviour which deviates from the acceptable framework arouses deep anxiety.[8] One finds a 'gender conscience' functioning. It is not biological destiny, but it has such profound psychological roots that gender deviation cannot be tolerated. In fact, gender identity seems to be fully established by the age of three. The stress and confusion involved in trying to change gender identity once it has been established lead many psychologists to suggest that if a sexual misdiagnosis has not been corrected by the time the child is eighteen months, then it is easier to perform genital plastic surgery than to relabel the child and have that child try to develop a new gender identity.

So it is during the first years of life that gender identity is established, and these years are usually spent in the care of the mother, or of a woman who substitutes for the mother. The most important task of the first three years of a human's life is establishing a close relationship with a caretaker. This is crucial to what we see as being a nonpsychotic human being. It provides us not only with the capacity to form relationships with others, but to gain knowledge of ourselves as individuals of value, who have some ability to act and survive within the world. During the first few weeks of life, and continuing to six or seven months, the infant behaves and feels as though she or he and the mother are one. It is generally thought that the infant views this system as omnipotent – there is on the one hand the infant with her/his pressing and ill-understood needs, and on the other hand, the reliever of those needs. Thus the infant, who is helpless, is not invaded with fear because she or he finds a powerful helper close at hand, so close that at first the caretaker is conceived as part of the infant's self. This security, however, comes at the expense of the self, and the infant's next task is to preserve the self by discovering his or her separation from the primary caretaker. His or her feelings, thoughts, characteristics, are now part of an individual identity. This task of separation and individuation begins in the first year of life, and is carried on to adulthood, and beyond.

The tasks of separation and individuation from the primary caretaker, who is almost always the mother, are often difficult, and there is no reason to suppose that men have an easier time of it than do women. Men often feel crippled by intense attachments to their mothers, and find their tentative efforts at control undermined by the mother's intrusive attachments. These difficulties caught the imagination of previous decades, aided by Philip Roth's fictional mothers. Today the focus is on the daughter's persistent and limiting attachments to her mother which may catch her up as she tries so hard to be different from her mother.

The process of separation, in the very early stages, involves 'practising', whereby the child tends to check back with his or her mother for reassurance. The child tests its own skills in movement and manipulation and sets off on its own to investigate things around him or her. But the child returns to the mother for what is called by psychologists 'refuelling' – a confirmed sense of home base gives the child renewed energy for further autonomous exploration and development. But the mother can easily interfere with the refuelling process. She can indicate that the child's forays into autonomy are fraught with danger. She can express displeasure or anxiety. She can punish the child for his or her independence by withdrawing approval. The child, after the initial euphoria in discovering his or her capacity to move, to explore, to develop, soon learns that there are limitations to this development. The mother, too, appears in a less grand and secure light; she has lost the omnipotence she appeared to have in the symbiotic stage. The child is therefore susceptible to doubts expressed or suggested by the mother's behaviour, and it is thought that mothers themselves have more difficulty endorsing daughters' attempts at independence. One theory is that the mother identifies with the daughter, and her own unresolved wishes from infancy are evoked. The mother sees the development from symbiosis as a betrayal; she responds to the symbiotic phase in her daughter and loses any sense of who is the mother and who is the child. The mother's confusion can easily infect the child, who is already ambivalent, for the child both wants to develop her autonomy and to return to the safety and confidence of the symbiotic stage. Girls do seem more prone to depression during the period of separation and individuation than do boys, and this is the period, too, when gender enters explicitly into psychological development. (Also, girls tend to display more dependence on their mothers in this phase.) No one knows why this is so. Does the girl recognise the mother's limitations as a woman in our society, and does she then see her own limitations as she identifies with her mother? Is she more sensitive than her male peer to the shift from the euphoria of discovering her skills to the frustration of not being able to do enough? Or does she suffer from penis envy, that legacy from Freud which persists like a ridiculous canker even in intelligent minds?

Penis Envy and Gender Identity

Ten years ago it was enough to call the theory of penis envy and its place in the psychological development of women 'patriarchal' – that alone condemned it. Juliet Mitchell, however, pointed out that we live in a patriarchal society, and that female psychology was bound to register this fact.[9] Freud's low opinion of women did not prejudice him. He simply did his best to record the effect of male chauvinism on women. Freud's story is that the girl's first love, like that of a boy, is the mother. When the girl discovers her 'castration', or the absence of a penis, she turns in horror from the mother (who shares this 'injury' or 'wound' and who is responsible for bringing her into the world thus deformed). The girl turns to her father, hoping that he will provide her with the penis she desires, but she can have a penis only temporarily, during sexual intercourse. She cannot have her father, but she can hope for a substitute man and, more importantly, she can look to a child which features in her mind as a substitute for a penis. Her greatest fulfilment will be found in a male child who will not only belong to her and have a penis, but who will also have access to the freedom, to the chances for mastery and development of which she has been deprived.

Whatever truth there ever was in Freud's account, it must be seen as a crude simplification of a woman's sense of herself and of what it is that men have which she lacks. She may envy man's freedom, his power, his privileges, and his penis may be a symbol of that. Or, like any child, a girl may envy a boy his penis simply because she does not have it, and this could mean no more than envying a child a toy she lacks. She could be dissatisfied with her life, with her prospects, and so envy a boy anything.

Freud understood the difference between sex and gender. He noted that little girls were every bit as bright, if not brighter, than little boys. He believed that the differences between male and female psychology were developed, not inborn. Yet somehow the male organ had an innate superiority which had a crucial impact on a young girl's development. And then to see motherhood as a compensation for 'lacking' a penis, as though it had no benefits in and of itself! He did indeed, as he recognised, have a good deal of trouble understanding women.

But girls do develop differently from boys, even though it is not clear that, in this early stage, when gender identity is forming, they are treated with any significant or systematic differences. There have been many studies of adult responses to different sexed infants. For a while it was believed that parents interpreted child's cries differently – a girl crying would be thought to be sad, and so would be comforted, whereas a boy crying would be heard to be angry, and so would stimulate anger in the parent who would tend to leave it alone more often. The girl, therefore, it was thought, did not learn to cope with discomfort. She learned instead to turn to other people. Also, it was thought – and this has been used in many feminist accounts of female development – that an adult is quicker to help a girl with a problem than a boy. Therefore the girl is encouraged to be more dependent. It was thought that girls were cuddled more, and therefore taught to need affection. It was also, in contradiction, thought that boys were handled more, and therefore had the advantage of more stimulation. Yet a recent and thorough study found no observable differences, according to gender, of parental warmth, reaction to dependence or independence, amount of praise or feedback. No gender differences could be found in a child seeking or receiving physical contact.[10]

But girls and boys do develop differently. They do, quite simply, establish a gender identity, and this has a great deal to do with how they identify with mothers and fathers, and how they resolve conflicts with their parents, or how these conflicts reach stalemate. Mothers do tend to see their daughters as more closely bound to them than their sons, or bound to them in a different way. The emergence from the symbiotic phase is less secure. Women tend, far more than men, to suffer from psychosis involving loss of self boundaries, and in normal life, too, they experience themselves in relation to others. A very interesting psychoanalytic theory, replacing Freud's account of penis envy, has been articulated by Nancy Chodorow in her book *The Reproduction of Mothering*. As long as women mother, daughters will develop a certain kind of relatedness to others which will prime them for mothering. Because girls are parented by a person of the same gender, they come to experience themselves as less differentiated than boys. The girl does not have to repress her attachment to the mother (as does the boy, through fear of punishment), and when the daughter does turn to the father she does not turn away from the mother, but is always looking back at her. According to Chodorow, the boy's inner world is more fixed and simple, because he has had to repress so much of his feeling for his mother. Masculine personality is based on a denial of connection and relatedness, whereas the feminine personality emerges from childhood with a basis for empathy built into the ego.

Envy of Mother

Here then is the positive aspect of female development, but how do we account for those cruel twists of gender development whereby the girl does not simply accept her dependency needs but also denies her expansive needs? A psychoanalytic account of this is given in Dorothy Dinnerstein's powerful but fantastic book *The Mermaid and the Minotaur*.

Daughters may be quick to perceive their mother's limitations, but boys may remember the time when the mother appeared omnipotent, and thus fear being engulfed by the mother, and therefore find themselves limiting women's power, or trying to contain that awful power. Why have women conspired along with men to demean women? Why have women accepted male domination? Why do they, who are presumably so empathetic, permit cruelty and aggression in their men? What is their part in the 'male' conspiracy?

Basing her theory of gender development not on an Oedipal theory but on Melanie Klein's article, 'Envy and Gratitude', Dinnerstein believes that the initial gratitude an infant feels towards his mother for her care and love, is accompanied by rage. The care can never be sufficient, the love never perfect. Dependence, when disappointed, arouses terrible rage, not only because of the frustration, but because it reminds the infant of his helplessness. Men forever fear that first powerful woman, from whom they wanted everything, upon whom they were totally dependent, who never gave them enough and from whom it was so difficult to emerge as a separate person. The industrial, rule-centred world is compensation for their helplessness, and their independence is a screen for their fear of symbiosis. Women support them in this facade because they too suffered from their mother's power. Doomed by sex to be mothers themselves, they have denied in themselves this similar awful power and so agree with men that woman has no power. This is better than identifying with that terrible first mother.

It is difficult to choose between these two currently accepted but contradictory theories. Chodorow sees gender as arising from the daughter's identification with the mother. Dinnerstein sees female gender as developing through a necessary denial of identification with the mother; women prefer to succumb to false dictators rather than see the demon in themselves. But the reason Chodorow's theory seems to be a tremendous advance in the psychology of women, is that it is not recalcitrantly negative. Daughters develop differently to sons; but the difference is not pure limitation. It may give rise to limitations, but these are like an imbalance, not a fraud on the entire female story. Explanations like Dinnerstein's deny that women have any genuine story to tell, other than that of oppression. They deny that women, devoting themselves to mothering, are doing something real, satisfying real needs, and that the trade-offs necessary to this kind of devotion make sense to mothers, though they may also lead to dissatisfaction, and though those trade-offs are necessary because we live in an unfair world. There seems to be a missing text to women's lives, a current censorship on their needs as mothers and on the personalities, the modes of thought, the attitudes that make mothering important to women.

Mother as Daughter

Even if we cannot accept the rigid psychoanalytic scheme of Nancy Chodorow's account of gender identity, we can make use of the assumption that gender identity develops as it does because the principle caretaker is a woman, whose influence is different upon girls and boys. Girls experience themselves as like their mothers – partly in response to the mother's tendency to encourage, or even enforce, symbiosis between herself and a daughter. Therefore girls tend to learn that attachment is accompanied by a fusing of identity. Their mother is their first love, and her love is symbiotic. Most women feel that they never become totally separate.[11] However independent they become, they are also aware of themselves as part of other people. Boys on the other hand define themselves in opposition to their mothers. They identify with their fathers, but their fathers tend to be more distant from them. Their fathers are strangers, or strangers in the language of childhood, whereby anything outside the self is strange. In seeing themselves to be like a father and not a mother, boys curtail their empathic tie with their primary love object. That is, they see themselves as different from the person to whom they were first attached, and most attached, and therefore the symbiosis they experience in the first stages of infancy does not form, so centrally, a part of their identity.

It is misleading, confusing and harmful to cling to this analysis as though it marked differences we could always see or which are always present even when we cannot see them. The distinctions I am making must be seen as matters of emphasis. Men are people too, with needs and capacities for forming attachments, and these attachments create dependencies and extend their identity to include the personalities and interests of others. It is alarming how frequently feminist arguments forget this, just as they forget the value to a woman of mothering. But for women, in general, their dependency and their response to others' dependence on them, has a greater tendency to take priority. This can be seen with remarkable clarity in the study of children's games.

Games, Gender and Maturity

Children's play is the work of a child. Fantasy becomes a wish for mastering a world in which one is largely helpless, and, at its best, will lead to practice, to skill, to knowledge. Games are the crucible of social development. They offer one important way in which a child can learn respect for rules and come to understand the way rules can be made and changed. It has long been noted that there are marked differences between the way boys play games and the way girls play games, and recent studies support the old findings.[12] Boys play outdoors more than girls. They play more often in large and varied groups. They play competitive games more often, and their games last longer.

What do these differences mean? What happens to end girls' games? Like all children, girls play games by rules, and like all children, girls fall out in arguments over what the rules are and whether they are being followed. But whereas boys will argue this out and punish offenders, girls tend to change the course of the game, go on to a different one, rather than fall out with the players. Their priority is to preserve good relations at the expense of the game,

41

whereas for boys the game comes first. Once we see this, we can understand why girls tend to play in smaller groups. If relating to the players is more important than the game played, then it is better to have fewer players, thus allowing one to be closer to each person. Their games might finish sooner, also, because with less elaborate rules, the games might be more boring. Or, because the player is more important than the game played, the game may be abandoned when sufficient contact has been made to approach the player directly.

Games show children's ability to utilise and develop rules. Is it not the case that girls are backward, compared to boys, when we consider this skill? Are they not, as Freud thought, lacking a firm sense of principle? Can we not see from this why moral argument is difficult with women, and why they always seem to be sliding away from the point?

It may be a long jump from girl's games to moral development, and from moral development to the question of why women mother, but there is a connection. Carol Gilligan, a Harvard psychologist, found that women use a different moral language.[13] Girls' games seem less well developed than do boys' games only if one takes boys' games as a standard of maturity and ignores the point and purpose of girls' games. It is far from clear that concern with rules over the feelings of others indicates greater sophistication, or that competition is a better skill than compromise. What psychologists are doing when they evaluate boys' and girls' games is to use boys' games as a standard, thus ignoring what the differences actually show.

Gender and Morality

Gilligan studied the different way boys and girls responded to moral dilemmas. A man's wife is dying and he has no money to pay the chemist, who refuses him the necessary medicine without payment. Is he justified in stealing the medicine? This dilemma shows up the cruelty of American health facilities, which are outrageously commercial, but it was only the girls who commented on the frame of the dilemma itself, who wanted to obliterate the context in which it occurred. The boys stuck to the rules of argument and weighed pros and cons of behaving in a way one would consider, normally, to be wrong. Yes, they said, the man would be justified in stealing the medicine even though in general stealing would be wrong. Girls, however, worried that the man would be caught – after all, he wasn't used to stealing and he might not be good at it – and then his wife would not only not have the medicine but would also be separated from her husband. Perhaps the husband should talk to the chemist, surely the chemist would understand and help him, or would lend him the money on a promissory note. The girls, it seemed, were less mature in argument. They wanted to change the context of the dilemma, rather than deal with the given terms.

Is it that women simply will not stick to the task at hand but at the same time want to change the world? Well, they do want to change things. They do refuse to accept certain alternatives. And they do speak a different moral language. For women, Gilligan found, the moral imperative is to care. The primary responsibility is to alleviate pain or distress. For men, on the other hand, the moral priority is to respect the rights of others. Thereby they assure themselves of certain rights, and noninterference in those rights. The morality of rights is centred on fairness, fairness in the sense of everyone being treated the same, whereas the ethic of responsibility acknowledges differences in needs. Women are therefore less well equipped than men to protect their own rights. They respond to the needs of others, and they try to act so as not to hurt others, or decide which action will cause others the least pain. The moral crises in their lives are characterised by the knowledge that it is sometimes impossible not to hurt someone – for them that tends to be the greatest dilemma, rather than one of opposing principles, which may in a given case have no relevance to either hurting or healing. Moral maturity for a woman comes when she sees the illogic, the inequality involved in thinking only of helping others. She is a person too. Therefore actions which hurt her must also be seen to be bad actions.

43

To use this realisation to deny the feelings of others, however, would be to ignore what she has already learned, to dismiss the truths of her moral language. Instead she shifts from thinking only of others to considering the rights and needs of herself as well.

Women mother because they tend to be better at it than men. They develop as people who will be particularly responsive to others and who will see themselves in relation to others. Fathers take the mothering role only when something overrides usual patterns and forces them to develop certain skills. Women mother because nurturing others, and giving up certain things in order to nurture, is a process which makes sense to them. They are accustomed, since childhood, to see themselves in relation to others. This is not a cheat, not a fraud practised upon them. It is a human reality. But it is also subject to distortion, and a mother's special sense of her children's needs, her identification with those needs, is encouraged to become distorted in the institution of motherhood wherein fathers become deprived of their children, of the chance to develop their parental skills and so let the burden fall wholly upon the mother. She may well respond to this pressure by becoming a full-time parent – or, if she tries to honour her expansive needs too, she may have to act and think like a man in the professional world, while bound to sympathy, consideration and care at home. She is like a double-visioned creature in a tunnel-visioned world.

3
What do the Children Need?

Mothers may be people, and therefore suffer the mixed blessings of complex needs, but what about the children? Do they not need, at least when they are small, full-time mothering – a mother's constant love and constant presence? If mothering is invented, surely it is invented by children. It is not a male, but a child's conspiracy that stresses the importance of the mother being at home, being available, being the constant companion, entertainer and comforter. Women of today, having married men of today, find their husbands want them to have other interests, to exercise other skills, but the child's grasping hands and bellowing anxiety keep her home and lock her in. The child, not the father, is the gaoler, and the child is only fighting for his rights.

Cost-Benefits of Full-time Mothering

Any full-time mother knows she is crippling herself by being a full-time parent, unless she is particularly lucky in having a flexible personality, and is able to put certain needs in abeyance, without an accompanying depression (though this is unusual: nearly half of British mothers who are confined to their homes with young children suffer from depression[1]) – but surely it is worth it, for the sake of the children? Penelope Leach claims that there is a cover-up now in progress. Everyone who knows anything about it knows that children are better off with their mothers at home, that in the care of a full-time mother children develop greater emotional maturity and their verbal skills develop more rapidly. Their general well-being depends upon the continuous presence of a mother, and there is no substitute for a mother.[2] These truths are denied, Leach believes, to save the feelings, to moderate the anxiety of those mothers who have to work, or want to work. Mothers are special, she claims, because without their full-time love, children never advance beyond having fleeting, indiscriminate interest in others; they never develop as people who form lasting attachments. Mothers are special, she notes, and children know this because even when they are looked after almost entirely by others, they show marked preference for and profound attachments to the mother they may see for only an hour a day. Well, who cares about contradictions when making points on behalf of the children?

Leach is the most recent in a long line of psychologists and doctors who cause mothers to tremble at the thought of pursuing their own needs. From Freud we learned that psychological distress was the fault of early training. Often he cited a father or a nurse or governess as the instigator of a trauma, but because his work became popular at a time when mothers alone tended to look after their children during infancy, mothers looked to themselves alone for causes of childhood distress and maladjustment. Enforcing their terrifying responsibility was John Bowlby's report to the World Health Organisation, which coincided with the popularisation of Freud's work in the 1950s. Bowlby studied the effects of maternal deprivation on children. His work was done in institutions caring for infants who had been orphaned, and in hospitals which at that time did not allow much contact between parents and child patients. When infants ranging from six to twelve months were separated from their mothers they displayed anxiety, crying, withdrawal, lassitude, dejection, insomnia, loss of appetite, weight loss and extreme slowness in growth and development. The syndrome is known as 'anaclitic depression' – depression stemming from the absence of anything to 'lean on'. In somewhat older children the effects of maternal deprivation were more clearly marked into three different phases. On first being separated from the mother, the child is restless and tearful. He appears to search for the mother, as though he really cannot believe her to be absent. This stage of protest gives way to the despair of recovering her. Yet he remains preoccupied with her and watchful for her return. Later, however, he gives up on finding her, and loses interest in her. He becomes in this third stage emotionally detached. The child shows no interest in anything around him, and even the mother's return is treated with indifference. The loss of the mother leads to an inability to retain any attachment, any interest. It stunts development; it crushes potential.

We have to be careful with our children. We care, terribly, about them, and we know that we are often unsure about what they need, what they are thinking, and what is best for their development. We can therefore easily be held hostage to such theories. Even if there is only a chance that they are true, then we should follow their recommendations. Our children only have one childhood.

Maternal Deprivation v. Temporary Absence

The big, glaring deficiency of Bowlby's studies is that he looked at children who were living in institutions, whose life patterns had been disrupted, who were deprived not just of their mothers, but of their fathers, of their entire families, of

domestic surroundings, of individual care. Bowlby looked at
children who were suffering from all kinds of deprivation,
and diagnosed them as suffering from maternal deprivation.

Anyone who looks at Bowlby's work can see this. His work
is important in showing us something of what children need.
They do not live by bread alone. They fail to thrive, fail to
grow, can even die, if they are not fondled, given that special
attention that parents naturally give them. They suffer not
only psychologically, but physically. And infants' primary
attachment is not, as was once thought, a cupboard love,
based on appreciation for being fed. It seems, instead, to be
based on a sense of physical contact, and the need to be close
to another body. This need appears to be a stronger force for
attachment than the need for food.[3] But is it the need for the
mother – or is it need for the kind of attention and handling
that the mother usually gives the child, but which could well
be offered by someone else, or shared by the mother, the
father, the grandmother, a housekeeper?

Children, like mothers, have both dependency needs and
needs for autonomy, or independence, allowing them not
only to develop a sense of separateness and individuality
but also to exercise that individuality, to expand it, to
stretch and master skills and perceptions. But, it is now
claimed by child psychologists, the worst thing a mother
can do when her child is developing an autonomous ego, is
to make herself unavailable to the child. A child's longing
for an unavailable mother tends to make him or her regress
to symbiotic longings, rather than to move forward to
further ego development.[4] To be independent the child
must first be dependent. To be independent the child must
have not only the approval but also the presence of the
person upon whom he or she is dependent.

But what precisely is necessary to the formation of attachment to the mother? What does making herself available mean? Bowlby looked at separations of several weeks
at least, but the popularisation of his work led women to
wonder whether it would harm their child if they went out
shopping for an hour or two. In fact, his conclusions have
no bearing upon working mothers, who are normally absent

for certain regular periods during the day and who regularly reestablish contact with their children. The working mother does not therefore disrupt her child's life patterns, or confuse him. It is possible for her to leave the child in good care, which will provide him with what he needs during his mother's absence. Even if a child loses his primary parent and is given institutional care, Bowlby's findings are not always reproduced if the care is good. He looked at substandard conditions. He looked at infants and children whose physical needs alone were attended to, who were deprived of special adult attention and handling. He looked at children who were in effect neglected, not simply deprived of their mothers.

Yet Bowlby's conclusions are still endorsed, and though the faults of his argument are widely known, they are ignored. In Leach's new diatribe against working mothers[5] she does not appeal to studies, to group observations, to experimental conditions, only to her own experience and her armchair theories of what is possible for children, and what is good for them. Since child-rearing and children form for her a professional focus of interest, she can stay happily at home, having her expansive needs endorsed because she can do her work at home, while telling other mothers that they have no pressing expansive needs and that their proper place is with the children. Like Phyllis Shlafly, whose life's work is to tell other women they should not work, who exhibits the viability of fulfilling a mission and being a mother at the same time, Leach denies the possibility she represents. According to Leach 'tiny gaps' in the company of the mother can be tolerated by the child, but even these are wounds which must heal. She recalls looking after a child for a day and being unable to interpret the child's whimpers and needs precisely. Did the child want to be cuddled, or did he need to whine himself to sleep? Did he want to clutch his blanket, or should it cover him? But of course it is not the mother alone who can learn these things. Anyone can get to know a child. Many adults, from fathers to nannies to grandmothers, are good at learning what a child wants and needs.

Women usually want to mother their children – that is, they want not only to bear children, but to care for them. This activity does take a special part in their lives. It is a genuine need, a genuine pleasure. And it is because of its genuineness that people can become so confused about it. If women had no particular relation to mothering, no particular talent for it, no special impulse towards mothering, then they could spot the sham and shake if off, as the feminists of the early 1970s expected. But because the pleasures of mothering and the need to mother are not shams, ideas which endorse them can overstate, confuse and yet seem true. Because of the profound part child-rearing plays in the lives of mothers, statements about the child's special need of the mother flatter her. The mother seems particularly good at understanding the child and interpreting his preverbal demands. The mother is then needed – and that is good, to have her own needs for children rendered useful. But it also traps her, and quite unnecessarily. The mother may be the first to understand and interpret, but she need not be the only one able to do this. She will be the only one, only if she is the only one who looks after the child regularly, for any length of time. Other people can learn to interpret the child's preverbal requests. The mother had to learn how to do it, and others can learn too, if only she lets them. If the mother wants to meet her other needs, then she will have to give up her position as unique interpreter and nurturer. It is a price to pay, but not too dear a price.

Children do not need to be cared for only by their mothers, or even primarily by their mothers. If a child is cared for only by his mother – and this would include the once typical arrangement whereby the father sees the child for an hour in the evening, and on weekends – then he learns to need only the mother. But it is an unnecessary need. A child functions very well with various people looking after him.[6] He needs continuity. He needs the same caretakers. But he does not need only one. In fact, it seems that a child feels more secure if more people look after him. A baby who is bathed regularly by his father as well as his mother shows less distress upon being separated from the mother. Naturally too many caretakers will confuse the child, but at a very young age he is able to distinguish between people and recognise them and has no trouble with as many as five or six people. There will be preferences, and these preferences are usually for the mother. She can relinquish her exclusive role, without relinquishing her special role.

Motherhood Reproduced

There is no question that the newborn infant requires individual, human care. The core of a healthy person develops only in the absence of overwhelming anxiety, and in the presence of continuing care, which involves holding, feeding and a relatively consistent pattern of interaction. Institutionalised children supplied with the necessary physical requirements but not provided with emotional relationships, are often unable to form relationships later in life. Indeed, many do not even develop basic motor and verbal skills. They may even fail to thrive physically, and die. Mothers tend to be the person who cares for the child, but mothers learn to do this, just as anyone else would. When mothers are not given the opportunity to learn, they are less good at it. Mothers separated from their premature infants for the first few weeks after birth tend to smile less at their infants, hold them less closely, and to touch them less affectionately than mothers of normal infants, or mothers of premature infants who were allowed to touch and hold their infants. Fathers' attachment behaviour has not been studied so carefully in this context, and only recently has there been much interest on precisely the effect fathers have upon children, or precisely what fathers' capacities for 'mothering' are, but they do react similarly to women to a baby's sounds of pain or pleasure (this was measured by pupil dilation), and I am sure there is a great deal of untapped nurturing ability in men. Margaret Meade mentioned, in the BBC documentary on her life, that when a man experiences an infant's grasping reflex on his finger, he is 'hooked'. A man can easily be drawn into the complex, concentrated empathy the child arouses in the mother. The father, after all, has as much biosocial reason to rear the infant, because his infant carries half his genes. Whatever genetic impulse to nurture the woman carries is not overwhelming, nor exclusive. But in men it is undeveloped, and if they are to change, not only attitudes but family structure will have to change, and this can only change slowly because even the next generation of men and women are being raised primarily by mothers.

So, as things stand, it is usually the mother upon whom the infant initially becomes totally dependent, and this sets up a self-perpetuating tale of women mothering. It is the mother's care, then, that must be consistent and reliable; it is the mother's absence that produces anxiety. The infant's earliest experience and development takes place within this relationship. From this exclusive bond stem the patterns, battles, images and expectations that make women who mother, and men who do not. The father, siblings and peers influence the developing child, but images of these people lag well behind that of the mother, and do not become so crucial to the psychic organisation of the self.

Children do not need a mother who is their exclusive caretaker. Even Bowlby, in his more recent work, admits that an infant may be more secure, and more skilled at forming attachments, if he has more than one 'attachment figure', that is, someone who cares for him and upon whom he learns to depend. Children need continuing care, but they also need to become independent, and the intense primary identification with a mother alone may impede development. The mother-image, too, remains powerful and threatening, because the mother alone threatened independence, and the mother alone was the figure upon whom the infant was dependent. Motherhood is a self-perpetuating institution. It is not merely a problem of separating fact from fiction, but of breaking a cycle. We have to start somewhere. Some necessity must push us forward. The necessity we have met with is the discovery of women's expansive needs, and the pressure on them that arises from this recognition. These needs were felt before, but given all sorts of different names and presented in a variety of disguises. Now that we see them for what they are, we must act to meet them. To meet them, we must change the image of motherhood.

What happens to children when we do this? The theory, the hope is that they will grow up with a less rigid idea of male and female roles in child care, that they will have fewer internal defences against a totalitarian mother. Men will not fear women, since their fear may stem from that primary image of a mother who alone could assuage their helplessness. Women will not believe that they as mothers must act in a way to meet those recalcitrant, endless demands they made upon their own mothers. Certainly greater participation by the father in child-rearing works. Certainly care by nannies works. The generations growing up from the 1850s to the 1930s are evidence of that, since the nanny was as common then as certain forms of motherhood are today. These changes work in the sense that they are as capable as any child-rearing practice of bringing about nonpsychotic adults, adults who are capable of loving and working. But there is that persistent slide back to mother, to leaving it to mother, and to mother's acceptance of the full burden. She is quick to take the responsibility, the stress, and to be the easy alternative when any other child-care plans go awry – when the nanny is ill, when the child is unwell, when the father has other commitments. The mother is never too tired, never under too much stress, never too preoccupied – unless she is clinically ill, either physically or mentally. This may be her only way out, because a mother who is normal remains the backbone of child care, and the care of children can never be put into cold storage.

Being a working mother is like walking up a slide. Always there is a tendency to slip back to where one started, with the children landing on one's back, or falling into one's lap, having them thrown at one, having them throw themselves at one. A child needs its mother. The mother feels this, and always responds to this pressure. But what becomes of the child when the mother does work? It is no

longer feasible to believe that the child is crushed psychologically, with no capacity for forming relationships. The
child needs its mother, but it does not need a mother who is
always by its side.

Maternal Benefits

But what about the beneficial effects of the attention she
gives the child? Perhaps the child does not need her for
establishing a reasonably healthy psychic structure, but
surely he needs her to develop his optimal intelligence?
What differences can we see in school achievement between
children of working and nonworking mothers?

It should be easy to discover this, but it isn't. Mothers
work for all sorts of reasons, in all sorts of jobs and professions, and these reasons may influence the emotional and
intellectual well-being of the child. The effects of divorce, of
single parenting, of separation, paternal unemployment,
poverty have to be separated from the effects of maternal
employment. For many years it was thought that there were
no measurable differences in children of nonworking
mothers and children of working mothers – at least when
all the other variables of class and income level and family
structure were accounted for. But recently we have seen
some startling and puzzling results.[7]

It was found that in black families the performance of
children, academically and intellectually (on IQ tests), was
higher in families where the mother worked full time. Indeed, black families and black women tend to show very
different results from white middle-class families. There is a
different myth of the superwoman in black culture. The
black superwoman is not a woman dressed for success, a
dynamo at the office and a kitten at home, but a more
familiar domestic dynamo, who keeps the family in order,
who is herself invulnerable to disease and weakness while
she minimises the weakness, the fecklessness of her men.
She represents the power of the workhorse, of practical wisdom and constancy. Her image is an inheritance of her
slave past, when the white man could make her both

worker and whore, because she was strong, she was sexy, and nothing would break her. It was an image that eased his conscience and which he made reality by breaking the men, by making the slave woman head of the family, by depriving the father of any true role, by depriving him of the privilege of responsibility to his children. The false black macho, aggressive, careless of feeling, sexy but un-emotional, has been derived not only in opposition to the white man's dismissal of him, but also as a confirmation of it. The black man's family ties are defunct; his home is temporary, and his only power is a mean, transient strength.

Children of black working mothers do better than children of nonworking black mothers. This is really not surprising. Any children, of any race, who are in the lower 20 per cent income level of their community have higher scores on mental maturity tests than do their peers, if their mothers work. The working mother, in such a family, raises the overall well-being of a very low-income family. Full-time employment raises the self-esteem of the mother, raises her hopes, gives her security, control, a sense of social movement, a wider vision. Her clear purpose in her work renders mundane tasks meaningful. When she has the opportunity for real success, a real career or profession, she tends to be more steadfast, more certain, more determined than her white peer.

Why shouldn't similar results be found in white middle-class families? The income level is probably raised by the mother's employment – though not always, because she will tend to spend more on child care, will be less able to ask neighbours for favours, will less readily accept unsupervised afternoons for her children. But, like the black working mother, she will have a better self-image, she will provide a more positive role model, she will think more positively about herself. And all these things do good to the child – the girl child, that is. Because it seems that in white middle-class families, the daughters benefit from the mother's full-time employment and the sons suffer.

Why should these different effects be evident? One

possibility is that the stimulation a mother gives her son is a great advantage. Teaching children is part of mothering, and in middle-class or upper middle-class families the mother is usually better equipped to stimulate children than the minder she employs. In America, and to a lesser extent in Britain, teaching very young children has become an obsession, and the mother stays home to do this. But why would this seem to benefit boys, and not girls? Is there still a prejudice in favour of teaching boys more than girls? This is a tempting conclusion, but there really is no evidence for it. There have been no observed differences in a mother's attitude towards teaching girls and boys, no difference in time spent, or attention given. So the explanation of the different effect is far more complicated.

Girls as well as boys benefit from the stimulation their mothers provide when they stay at home with them. Girls as well as boys suffer from a decrease in cognitive stimulation, at home, when their mothers work full time. But for a daughter there are considerable and overriding benefits as well. Is it genetic – are boys more vulnerable than girls to adverse environmental effects, or do they make more of stimulation at a certain age? No, because it was only in middle-income families that boys suffered where girls prospered, not in low-income families. In low-income families the boys did not suffer from full-time maternal employment – but, presumably, male genes are the same, or follow the same patterns, in middle- and low-income families. Well, a girl has a more positive role model. This may override negative effects. It may make her want to succeed. It may free her from that awful fear of success, which does seem to plague women, the complexities and deviousness of which I will discuss in another chapter. It is possible, too, that the image of the working woman is bad for the son, that it undermines the father's position, and so undermines his role model. Is there an inevitable see-saw between the sexes, so that a strong woman suggests a weak man?

No. The more positive women become, the more positive men can become too. The greater the maturity of the individual, the less he or she will conform to stereotyped sex roles. But there are differences between the sexes, and, in particular, there are differences between boys and girls, in the rate and patterns of development. Everyone knows that girls have a head start over boys, and some feminists think they then fall behind because they are impeded by one thing or another – and this is true, they often are impeded, but it is not the whole story, and it is a biased one

If mothers are worse at letting go of their daughters than of their sons, if the symbiotic tie between mother and daughter is so strong, and such a force in explaining why daughters grow up to mother their children themselves, then relief from the intense bond, and a better chance at independence, may encourage their intellectual development far more than does immediate maternal stimulation. Sons may, in the normal course of events, be granted just the right amount of independence, but when their mothers work full time, they may have too little supervision. The son's greater independence may amount to deficient attention, whereas the change in intensity, the thrust towards independence may, for the daughter of a working mother, be just right. But we must also consider the possibility that, during some stages of childhood, academic and intellectual achievement are not the goods we should strive for on behalf of our children, that this type of success may stem from personal inhibitions – in particular, it may stem from a desire to please, a fear of not pleasing, and a self-imposed limitation on psychological development. Boys who have been cared for exclusively by a mother for the first five years of life were found to internalise adult standards,[8] especially in regard to self-control and academic achievement. It could be that boys who are exclusively mothered become in this respect more like girls, and show a precosity similar to that of girls – a precosity which may eventually limit their horizons in that their aim is not to fulfil themselves but to please others. However, for boys this may be a less limiting task than it appears to be for girls because a boy pleases by being independent, adventurous and successful, whereas a girl, typically, does not.

Contradictory Conclusions

Mothers are hostage to theories. Their special link with their children's needs makes them so. And most studies of the effects of working mothers on children have assured people that children do not suffer when their mother works. But they also show that working mothers found more time for their children by foregoing more demanding jobs, working part time and eliminating personal leisure time. In fact, they found that working mothers spend almost as much time with their children as do nonworking mothers.[9] Nor was it found that fathers spend more time with their families if the mothers work. The superwoman syndrome was protecting the children and limiting the careers of the mothers.

Three months after one apparently definitive study was released, which 'proved' that children suffered no ill effects if their mothers worked, a new American study funded by the Department of Education contradicted the previous findings by the National Institute of Education. In white, two-parent homes, school students whose mothers worked full time during their school years scored up to nine percentile points lower on tests than students whose mothers never worked. The magnitude of the effect was directly related to how much the mother worked. Part-time working mothers' children scored better than full time, and the amount of time the mother worked was directly related to the relative highness or lowness of the child's score.

It is easy to point out the bias of this type of study. In her book *What Shall We Do with the Children* Judith Hann quotes a study which found that 98 per cent of a cross section of juvenile offenders were without a father or father substitute, but only 17 per cent were without a mother. Why not publish the effects of father's absence? Yet there is no doubt that the effect of absent fathers does not work the same way. Fathers say, 'Yes, it is a pity I have to leave my family, but there is this and this to consider', and they have no doubt they are right to do so. Even the fact that it is the effect of maternal employment that is studied, and that maternal employment is indicated as the cause of lower test results, rather than maternal employment in conjunction with a negligent father, indicates a bias in the study itself. The 'problem' (maternal employment) is named before the effects are known.

We are doomed, for the present however, to look at things this way, to worry about the effect of maternal employment on children, and to accept as a fundamental, unchangeable and reasonable part of life the effects not only of paternal employment but of paternal neglect on children. The first and most important bond is to the mother, and the child's psychological well-being depends upon his ability to obtain comfort from her, to hold her interest, her love, and to repair the sense of loss with her, which he has suffered in her absence. It will take a long time for things to change, and the change will be moderate, not revolutionary. The capacity to mother, the desire to mother, may well have some genetic foundation, enforced by psychological development within the institution of motherhood. As more mothers work, as more mothers devote themselves to work, more daughters will learn they can mother and work. It may be that sons will suffer for a while, and some daughters too. But women must continue to work in spite of this. The evidence of harm is slim, and nine points either way on a test result are not something at which to tremble. Mothers must care about what they are, too. They must try to meet all their human needs, all those needs that are well within reason, and which point to what we understand as human fulfilment. They must do this even if it costs their children a little. Because eventually their children will benefit. The daughters may learn how to be mothers and workers without being superwomen, and the sons may learn to expect a little less of women as sympathisers and dependants, and to develop more of their parental potential. Changes in attitudes are not enough. New ideas are not enough. If we want to proceed as women and workers without committing some form of emotional suicide, we have to accept that there will be conflicts, and that these conflicts are not shams, or the result of a conspiracy, but the result of complex needs within a society that has not as yet attuned itself to these particular complex needs. The children need us to work for this. This is what the children need.

4
Why Women Fail

Achievement v. Ability

It was found, about thirty years ago, that there was a reasonable correlation between a man's IQ and his adult accomplishments. His intelligence seemed to have some meaning. It did some work for him. He assessed his intelligence and allowed it to suggest certain goals. He was motivated to achieve his potential, and he valued his achievement. In the case of women, however, there was no relation between their intelligence and their achievement. Women with IQs of 170 and more were housewives or office workers.[1] Some were tickled by the idea of displaying a high intelligence on a test, but they did not consider this as a reason to devote themselves to anything other than husband, home and children.

Virginia Woolf draws a picture of Shakespeare's sister, a young woman of genius equal to that of her brother, but who, in trying to make her fortune in London, is degraded

61

and finally destroyed by a series of disasters peculiar to
women. She is seduced, impregnated, humiliated and hus-
banded. She has no future outside that of a wretched woman's lot, and her lot is particularly wretched because she
had the pride of genius, and left the safety, security and
limitations of her father's home to seek achievement and
fulfilment.[2]

But it is not only the conspiracy of society which teaches
women to be wary of ambition. There are more subtle
threats to her, threats to her femininity, to her capacity for
human attachment, to her happiness. In the film *Network*
Faye Dunaway plays a successful woman – successful, ambitious and therefore mean and lonely. We see men like this
in films, of course, men who like Citizen Kane are removed
from human warmth by wealth, or who must destroy their
careers if they are to embrace personal values and get the
woman they love, like Jack Lemmon in *The Apartment*, who
takes his doctor's advice and becomes a *mensch*, thereby
turning his back on the corrupt clique of man colleagues
and, accordingly, plunges to the lowest rung in the professional ladder. Men as well as women are sometimes slow to
see the rules of the game. Men as well as women are out-
raged by personal sacrifices necessary to certain types of
success, and men as well as women may refuse to make
those sacrifices, discovering in themselves unexpected needs
and priorities. Women do not have a monopoly on conflicts
between personal needs and professional ambitions. But
they seem to be aware of these conflicts from the beginning,
or rather, they seem more adept at avoiding them, than are
men. For the true tragedy of Shakespeare's sister is that in
all probability she does not even start out to London. She
does not harbour ambitions, and she does not discover her
genius. She knows the rules beforehand. She knows ambition will be punished. If she had the gumption to challenge
this knowledge by setting off for London, then in all probability she would not have been seduced. She would have
shrugged off rape. She would have continued to work with a
babe at her breast. If she had had the strength to acknowledge her own needs, she would have done a better job of

fulfilling them. She might have become mean and lonely, but only after she had got something of what she wanted. The real tragedy is that her defeat is self-inflicted, that she doesn't have a chance because she doesn't give herself a chance.

Success and Punishment

Success is something we normally think is desirable. We are expected to aim for it, and to welcome it. But clearly it is not that simple. What if we think we are bound to fail? Wouldn't it be better not to try, than to have our inadequacy proved? Or perhaps we do try, but something goes terribly wrong, not so much with the outcome but with our attempt. Some people, clearly, are out to defeat themselves, perhaps because they feel they do not deserve success, or because they are charting, unconsciously, means of self-revenge, self-punishment or punishment of others – such as parents or spouses – who care deeply for their well-being. But there is a different phenomenon seen in women. It does not occur only in women, or in all women, but it is a common female trait. And that is fear of success. This is not a desire for self-defeat or self-punishment. It is a fear of what success will do to them, and what they will have to suffer if they are successful. It is a rational fear, then, because it is based upon an assessment of consequences.

In 1969 the Harvard psychologist Matina Horner first reported results of research on fear of, or anxiety about, success among bright, high-achieving women.[3] She had first observed that certain situations in which achievement is measured, and measured in a competitive way, are more anxiety-provoking for women than for men. She tried to measure this phenomenon by asking a group to complete a story which began: 'After first term finals, Anne/John finds her/himself at the top of her/his medical school class.' The female members of the group were asked to complete the story about Anne's success, and the men were asked to fill in the details of John's success.

The men's stories primarily indicated happiness, satisfaction and a sense of earned achievement. 'John is a conscientious young man who worked hard', the story went. 'John has always wanted to go into medicine and is very dedicated . . . He continues working hard and eventually graduates at the top of his class.'

The women's stories, however, were often bizarre, full of unhappiness, anger and rejection. 'Anne starts proclaiming her surprise and joy', one story read. 'Her fellow classmates are so disgusted with her behaviour that they jump on her in a body and beat her. She is maimed for life.' The negative imagery was violent. Punishment was certain to follow. Fears were usually not so much of physical harm, however, as of social rejection ('Anne is an acne-faced bookworm. She runs to the bulletin board and finds she's at the top. As usual she smarts off. A chorus of groans is the rest of the class's reply . . .'). Also, there were fears that such success indicated abnormality, was an affront to femininity, and therefore to happiness as an adult female: 'Anne no longer feels certain she wants to be a doctor . . . she decides not to continue with her medical work but to take courses which have a deeper personal meaning for her.' Finally, there were cases in which Anne's success was denied – one woman completed the story as though it were really Anne's boyfriend who had come out on top, and another suggested that 'Anne' was the code name of a nonexistent person created by medical students who took turns writing exams for 'Anne'.

A full 65 per cent of the women Horner studied indicated some fear of success in their stories, in contrast to 10 per cent of the men. But these were, after all, only stories. Was there any relation to a person's performance, and the extent to which fear of success imagery was used in the stories? Horner went on to see whether there was any relation to fear of success imagery and behaviour one could call success-avoidant. She tested people first in competition with others, and then alone. She found that women who showed marked fear of success in their stories scored lower when they were tested in a competitive setting – especially when they were competing with men – and better when they were tested in solitary conditions. They worked better alone than in a group. They worked better when their work was not seen to compete with someone else's.

These results were devastating to the feminist image. Here was proof that it was not men who held women back, but women themselves. They chose not to compete. They were not good at competition. They feared the fruits of success. But though Horner's work is obviously an important contribution to the psychology of women, it is not altogether clear what it means. The women who displayed most fear of success had chosen fields thought suitable to women. All those she studied were intellectually talented, but not all were ambitious. Those who were humanities students and planning careers such as teacher or housewife, revealed a strong fear of success, whereas those women who were studying maths and physics, and who planned graduate degrees and careers in the sciences, showed relatively little fear of success. It is what one would expect. Those who feared success, avoided success. But it could also be that the women who showed Anne suffering rejection and loneliness and despair were inflicting these sad things upon her not because they actually expected her to suffer from them but because they wanted her to suffer them. Perhaps they were jealous of her success, rather than fearful of it. Perhaps they saw how their own lives were limited, how they themselves, in spite of intelligence and potential, had limited their vision, and were therefore angered by someone who was successfully pursuing higher goals. Perhaps they were not envisaging punishment to themselves, should they become successful, but were seeking envy's revenge upon another because she had surpassed them. Perhaps their 'fear of success' imagery was a display of competitiveness, not a denial of it. The women who had higher goals showed less violence towards Anne because they had less reason to envy her.

'Failure' is a Nice Girl

The nagging pressure to please may alienate us from our own needs. As a result we become dependent upon others for self-esteem, for self-definition. It is a vicious cycle – a woman devotes herself to others and, frustrated by lack of fulfilment of her expansive needs, she seeks compensations and assurance from the fulfilment of her dependency needs. This takes the form of dependence upon the needs of others, and upon their recognition of her fulfilling their needs. Thus we see women who enforce others' dependence upon them, because they themselves are lost without it. They fear the positive self-assertion that accompanies most types of achievement, and so they make requests and seek rewards in a roundabout way – but if these roundabout requests are to be met, then people must be responsive to their needs, even to the extent of feeling indebted to them. A woman may shiver, instead of closing a window, expecting someone else to notice her discomfort and close it for her. When she wants a cup of tea, she may ask everyone else if they want one, hoping to have the excuse of serving another rather than directly going for what she wants. She cannot therefore admit to her own needs, or be seen to put them first. The fear of success, in so far as it is the fear of social rejection, or of stepping out of a suitably feminine persona, is crippling. Nothing is gained, for her or for anyone around her.

It is often a long way on the road to meet one's true needs – though the way is now becoming less lonely. Fellow travellers help enormously, but we start alone, in the loneliness of our family, when a mother may instil in her daughter a fear of doing better than she has done. The mother may say, 'Do better than me. Don't be as I am', but her example is far more important than anything she says. The mother's self-denigration may infect the daughter, and the mother may not want her daughter to surpass her, not really. Dissatisfied people are good breeding-grounds for envy, and nothing defeats one's family as much as envy of them. The dissatisfied mother will lose her daughter if her daughter becomes strong and independent. Her daughter's success may confirm her own meaninglessness. Her daughter's success will prove that her self-limitations were unnecessary, and so she must prevent her daughter's success by teaching her daughter to fear success.

Fortunately there are ways of achieving success and yet denying one has it. Nancy Friday, author of *My Mother, My Self*, related how she always felt she was a fraud, that any success was somehow a trick she had pulled off, and that one day she would be found out. It is a neat attempt to see oneself still in a modest light, while enduring success. 'The real me has achieved nothing, but some sleight of hand has convinced others that I have.' She therefore does not allow self-denigration to get the better of her performance. Also, a successful woman can deny she had anything to do with her success. Katherine Graham, publisher of *The Washington Post*, declared, 'I still don't believe it. It's luck. I know it's girlish to say that.' Rita Hunter, the Wagnerian soprano, said, 'I can't believe I'm really singing leading Wagnerian roles now. I think I'm going to wake up and find it's all a dream.' Of course, luck does play a part in any person's success, but women more than men are quick to attribute success to luck, or to another external source – it has little to do with them.[4] On the other hand, they tend to blame their failures upon internal resources, such as lack of ability. Clearly this sometimes allows a woman to be successful without suffering anxiety about her femininity – and, I suppose, the anxiety about her 'being found out', or having her luck change, or waking up from a dream is less self-defeating than letting one's performance lag behind one's potential. Yet these attitudes can – though obviously they do not always – diminish one's chance of achievement. If one has lower expectations of success then, generally, one will do less well. If one is self-confident then one will have greater expectations of success. But if one believes that any success one has is due to luck, then even achievement will not enforce self-confidence. Some women get away with thinking achievement has nothing really to do with them, but it is a treacherous line to take.

The Emptiness of Success

Fear of success, and fears about success and the consequences of success, often lead to self-sabotage and stem from self-denigration. But is this the whole story? Can we not view it in more positive terms, as a rejection of the usual egoism that accompanies certain kinds of success? For some reason many women, including many of the very successful women I interviewed for this book, were reluctant to describe themselves as ambitious, or, if they accepted their ambition, they modified it. Sarah Weddington, who was President Carter's special adviser on women, sees herself as ambitious, but insisted on redefining ambition. 'It is an indication of an attitude that causes you to prepare yourself. But I don't like the part of the word that connotes using or hurting others.' Joan Cooney, president of Children's Television Network and creator of 'Sesame Street', declared that she was 'ambitious for my project, but not for myself'. Pam Hill, a documentary producer for the American television network ABC, said, 'I'm ambitious, yes, but I don't like it being said about me that I'm tough.' Anne Smith, managing editor of *Redbook* said, 'I'm ambitious, but not manipulative.' Even when women acknowledged their professional aims, their professional ambitions, they stepped away from the full, usual implications of the term. These women, who could not be said to fear success, or at least clearly did not fear success so much as to avoid it, eschewed the personality that typically accompanies ambition. In fact Playboy Vice-President Michelle Urry relates how she cried when people said she was tough and ambitious, even though she knew they were thereby complimenting her work.

Are these women indicating conflicts about success, and the ambition which is necessary to certain kinds of success? Or are they seeing a more complete picture of themselves? They are successful professionals, but they are people too. They need to be satisfied with their treatment of others. They need to be aware of their kinship with others and they need to see themselves as being fair and even kind. They are not necessarily caught up in a false female stereotype which dictates that a woman should not step out of her passive or compliant role. They are responding to a different conception of ambition. These women see the emotional costs at which success is often achieved, and though they value success, they want to integrate it with other things, equally important. Many women may have responded negatively to 'Anne's' test results because they saw something wrong with success defined in terms of getting better grades than someone else, and therefore putting someone else down.[5] Women may be ambivalent about competition, and therefore score better when they work on their own. Only when competitiveness is integrated into a meaningful vision, so that one is ambitious for a project, or ambitious to make a better life for one's children, or for the world, does it work. Things are changing, and more and more women are becoming ambitious for themselves, but still, though this is embraced by advertisers as the 'new woman' image, and decried by Betty Friedan as the feminist mystique, it is a highly superficial image, a temporary personality, and one that I simply did not find among the working mothers I interviewed. More and more women were keen to fulfil their expansive needs, but there was less of the hard fighting spirit of the 1970s. That rush of egoism had subsided with the pressures, pleasures and profundities of motherhood. If these women were ambitious, they were also capable and concerned, and needed to see themselves as such.

Success Reconsidered

The first attempt to define and then to measure fear of success had a great impact on the psychology of women because it confirmed the existence of attitudes and conflicts women feared in themselves. The image of femininity is of a person ready to please – not threaten, startle or impress. It is of someone who is well liked, and ready to serve others' purposes before her own, or who makes others' purposes her own. But the first results have not been reproduced in other tests, and there are certain marked differences found in similar studies. First, it was found that when the subjects studied were black, the men showed a stronger rate of fear of success than the women did. Black women have had the dubious advantage of learning that other people will not look after them, that they cannot depend on other people to earn money for them and their children. The double jeopardy of being both black and female makes a stronger, more positive woman, who is not afraid of success, who is not afraid of being a fighter. But she has, unlike the white woman, a clear context in which to see her ambition. It is definitely for something – for a better way of life for her children, for presenting an example of what a black woman can be. She is readier than her white peer to acknowledge her anger, her toughness and her ambition. Her sense that other people are bound to hurt her makes her less afraid of the effect her ambition and competitiveness may have. And black men may fear success more because they will be spurned by their peers who have not made it, played the white man's game and learned the white man's rules. But more recent studies show that white middle-class men, too, are more frequently displaying signs of fear of success, or aversion to success, because they have learned to see the cost of success. Men, too, fear being alone, they fear missing out on intimacy, and of being bereft of their children's childhood. They are learning to value it, as do women.

Fear of success is not purely negative. The ambivalence about success may stem from a wider awareness, rather than self-limitation. It is certainly not a simple, single phenomenon. It is not simply a matter of women being afraid to step out of a feminine role, and it is not merely a sign of women's envy towards others who have achieved success. But even though it has positive aspects, it is an area which indicates conflict and ambivalence, and therefore it can be self-defeating. If it is, then a high price is paid to avoid the anxiety accompanying success – a price paid in feelings of frustration, hostility and bitterness. It can lead to that awful sense of having cheated oneself out of an important part of one's life, of being duped by ideas one does not really believe in. But many fears suggest that fear of success can actually be an impetus to success. Barbara Walters said that for years she was afraid that she would simply disappear from her profession. She feared she would never get another assignment, that she would be forgotten. This anxiety about her success, her inability to believe that she really was successful and her uncertainty in being able to compete with others for a job, made her work harder, made her constantly present new ideas to the producers, forced her to develop a style and professionalism all her own. Now she admits that she believes when she wakes up in the morning she will find that she is 'still there' in the sense of still having a viable career. This certainty cost her much anxiety, and her determination may have cost her a marriage or two, but she confronted the anxiety, she lived with it, and she made it work for her. Often women do have to work harder than any man to get ahead. Often they do have to be better than any man to get job. But often the push towards excellence comes from the knowledge that they may undermine themselves, that if they are not very careful something may go wrong with their efforts. They will be sidetracked. They will allow priorities to shift. They will forget the masculine rules of the game, which look to winning, to competition, and forget their own rules, which are often called 'immature' because they put affiliative needs first and get out of the running rather than hurt others or impair their relations with others. Is it naïvete, as so many feminists have thought? Is it weakness and blindness? Or is it a rejection of shallowness, and a more complete view of what a person is, and what a person needs? Unfortunately, if it is the latter, then this greater awareness does not always lead to greater satisfaction. The simple-minded are better at getting what they want. They see only one thing at a time, and fasten upon a single goal. A girl who stops playing a game because she sees what is happening to her friendships as she plays the game, is not less mature, less determined, than a boy who plays according to the rules and accepts the contest and its consequences. She will not be as good at winning, however, unless the rules of the game change and we set up a new sense of what it is to win.

The successful women who claimed they were ambitious, but with a difference, were trying to do this.

5
Depression – A Female Ailment?

Twice as many women as men are treated for depression. Twice as many women attempt suicide. Depression and despair are women's problems, aren't they?

What is Depression?

Depression is different from unhappiness. Unhappiness centres around a defect in one's life that can be named. We are unhappy about our marriage, our job, our children's future. Or perhaps our unhappiness is a mood. We feel 'down' or 'blue'. We pass in and out of such moods, but we continue to function well enough. We may be dissatisfied with certain people close to us, or with certain conditions of our lives, but we have sufficient control over ourselves and our lives to deal with or at least to cope with these problems. The depressed person, however, does not only suffer from depressed moods. He or she also suffers profound disruption of normal functioning, and may experience insomnia – or

72

perhaps excessive sleep, escaping stress by avoiding all stimulation – loss of appetite, whereby one wishes oneself annihilated, or does not feel one deserves nourishment, or excessive eating, whereby one takes a vicious delight in making oneself gross. Depression is characterised, too, by loss of energy, decreased interest in one's usual activities, or indeed, in all activities, including sex. It is usually accompanied by slow or confused thinking, recurrent thoughts of death or suicide, lowered self-esteem and self-reproach. Indeed, the depressed person sees himself or herself as the centre of unhappiness, and as its source. Life is wrong, because one has made it so, or because one is trapped within oneself and must live life through oneself. The depressed person is rarely aggressive because he or she sees little point in lashing out at others. The faults are felt to lie within, and the victim is oneself.

Many people are depressed, but not treated for depression. Could it be that women more often than men have treatment? After all, if an employed man seeks help he must give up time from his work, sacrificing productivity. A woman who is unemployed, however, does not value her time in the same way, and may welcome treatment, or hospitalisation, as a change. This may in fact be the only way she can take a vacation from her work – that of being a housewife and mother. A woman who is depressed may have more confidence in authority. She may expect official help to be effective, or she may be more used to seeking help, or less ashamed to admit that she needs help. And, unlike men, women attempt suicide as a means of seeking help. Although twice as many women as men attempt suicide, 70 per cent of successful suicides are men. Women's attempts, therefore, fail either because they are ignorant about weapons, or because their despair is half-hearted. They believe that help is possible, if only someone will understand how badly off they are.

It is possible, too, that the sex ratios of depression are all wrong because a wide enough view is not taken about the manifestations of depression. Alcohol use and abuse, for example, are considerably higher in men. Do men who are reluctant to admit depressive feeling, or to seek help, 'drown their sorrows'? Could it be, too, that depression is the anger of a person who sees herself as having no power, and criminality is the anger of someone who has no acceptable power within society, and that the same impotent anger is expressed in depressives and criminals? In one case the anger is visited upon oneself. In the other it is turned outward, perhaps randomly. Do women end up in hospital wards and men in criminal courts for the same reasons? And indeed, as women become more like men, their symptoms may be changing. The rates of alcoholism, completed suicides and crime in women have now begun to rise.[1]

Depression and Lost Relationships

Even if various male-dominated illnesses – such as alcoholism and criminality – are eventually shown to be offshoots of depression, the question remains as to why depression in its present recognisable form bears such close relation to women, to their needs and disappointment. Genetic research has suggested that depression may be transmitted by an X-linked dominant gene – that is, it would be a genetic trait passed on to women twice as many times as to men. The more popular assumption is that depression – certainly the form of depressive moods – is a result of hormone functions, and women's hormones change in ways to make them susceptible to depression. But though depression is linked to certain hormones, it seems that these hormones are secreted by patients because they are depressed – not vice versa. And even if depression were a hormonal condition, it would not account for the role it plays in our lives. Whatever else depression is, it is clearly also a psychological condition involving a sense of loss, a loss of something within oneself that diminishes interest, hope and self-esteem. A depressed person can find no meaning or importance in her environment. Nothing confirms her value. Typically, she has no faith in her ability to change things for the better. Often she cannot even envisage an improvement. Depression is like bereavement in

74

that something valued is lost, out of reach. But bereavement is natural, normal and necessary, and it usually improves of its own accord. The lost person or relationship cannot be restored, but compensations can be found and new interests gradually discovered or old ones restored. In depression, however, the loss is within oneself, and there is a giving up on oneself. Even if the world changed, the depressive feels that her world would not change. Sometimes depression, like bereavement, is self-limiting. Sometimes people spontaneously recover. But while one is depressed one has the sense that nothing ever will be better, and that nothing could make one better.

This prevailing sense of loss in depression has made some people think that depression is about loss. In men as well as women a history of losses, or exit-type events, whereby someone close to the person abandons his or her life, through death, divorce, circumstantial separation (as in wartime) or simply through a withdrawal of affection, makes one more prone to depression. Maggie Scarf, in her book *Unfinished Business,* reported that every case of depression she found was precipitated by a loss. Women, Scarf concluded, were more susceptible to depression because they felt losses more deeply, because adult losses created echoes of previously unresolved or broken relationships, reverberations which were particularly devastating to women and relatively trouble-free to men because women have greater affiliative needs. 'When I began to gather material for this book', Scarf says, 'it was to be about the problem of women and depression. The book that I have written is, however, simply a book *about women.*' The story about depression becomes the story about women.

The trouble with Scarf's theory is that the women who are most at risk, in terms of depression, are not women who are in fact alone. The greatest threat to women is not divorce, separation, being widowed or having one's children leave home. The largest number of cases of depression occur among women who are married, with children living at home.

Yes, depression involves a sense of loss, but that loss

involves a loss of self, a loss of interests and of feedback that will reinforce the self. When we compare cases of depression in men and in women, we can see precisely what type of reinforcements are needed to waylay depression. Men who are unmarried suffer in a way that makes them prone to depression – not women. Women are particularly good at adapting to being alone (though they may, irrationally, fear it more). Women are adept at surviving the death of their husbands. Husbands increase stress, not emotional security. The widower's bereavement, however, does put him at greater risk. The divorced man is the one prone to depression. There is only one condition under which married men are as prone to depression as married women – and that is when they are unemployed.

Depression and Unemployment

Women, of course, are overrepresented among the unemployed. Not that they do not work, but they have no alternative role, which can support one's spirits, or at least offer distraction when something goes wrong in the domestic sphere. Even a tedious, mundane job outside the home offers opportunities for companionship. When the job outside the home is a good one, it will offer opportunities for success of a kind which provides confidence in other areas. The discovery that one can meet a challenge in one area reduces conflict and stress and fear in other areas, however unrelated they appear to be. A person who stutters, for example, may experience an alleviation of speech difficulties after his or her first successful parachute jump. Personal rejections, previously found humiliating, may be shrugged off after meeting a successful challenge.[2] Are women more prone to depression because their life-styles normally exclude them from the antidotes to depression? Like unemployed men, they have few reinforcers in their environment. They tend to be bound not only to a small sphere of movement (prescribed by the necessity of taking children with them), but to a small circle of relationships. They tend to feel underemployed, even when their attentions are constantly engaged by their children and by household tasks. A 'happy' marriage does not protect a woman from depression. A 'good husband' does not fulfil her needs, though presumably he goes some way towards fulfilling her affiliative needs. But affiliative needs are not enough.

Housewives are considerably more depressed than working wives, but working wives are still more depressed than working husbands.[3] A woman's double role creates a different kind of stress, and it is usually this stress, and the knowledge that there is bound to be such stress, that keeps many women as housewives, and makes many working women return to the home. Most working wives do nearly as much housework as nonworking wives. A working woman is still probably primarily responsible for the home. Whereas a man tends to relax when he comes home from work, a working mother returns to face other pressures – that of getting the home in order, arranging meals, bedtimes, planning for tomorrow, not only for herself but also for the other members of the household. But this cannot be the whole story. It is too slick – and there has been no correlation found between the amount of housework done and depression.

The predominance of depression which persists in working wives is more likely to come from anxiety about what she should be doing, what course her life will take. Today women are more aware of choices, and this will produce anxiety. When people see that their lives could be improved, they are more likely to become aware of dissatisfaction, to name the dissatisfaction, and to see life limitations as their responsibility. They see other women expanding their horizons. They now, to a greater extent, have social permission, or at least peer permission, to be other than a housewife, to set their goals high, even at the expense of their families, and at the expense of family harmony. They are more apt, now, to get social and peer permission, but they themselves are left alone with the profound conflict between the need to be with their families, to nurture them, and the need to expand their abilities and interests, and to have a fair shot at independence.

The harm that theories like Maggie Scarf's do, is to increase women's confusion. Most of us know that we are, in the 1980s, particularly prone to confusion about priorities. We need our children. We cannot deny that, though the women's movement, at first, sought to deny it. Raising children was a non-occupation. Children did not need to be brought up. They grew up all the same, declared Germaine Greer in *The Female Eunuch*. So women were left out in the cold with their maternal passions. If they were more prone to depression because they had greater need of others, then the need was a weakness. They need others because they have no self. The considerable positive aspect of work like Scarf's asserts the legitimacy of dependency needs, but unfortunately it romanticises these needs. Women are more profound, more sensitive because they are vulnerable to others, because emotional bonds have more meaning to them. Well, maybe this is so. Women, as I have argued, are better equipped to mother. There may be good bioevolutionary reasons for why mothering falls to them. There are good reasons, but not recalcitrant ones, not reasons which will never change, or should never change. But the real difficulty is not in learning how to live according to the demands of our affiliative needs, but how to live with these and to fulfil ourselves in other areas, too.

Learned Helplessness

The loss suffered in depression concerns a loss of self, but not simply the loss of a relationship or the loss of one's value to others. In the past few years the most fruitful work on depression has focused on the concept of learned helplessness, and the views of the self – as impotent, as worthy of abuse, as assuming a negative place in the world. This notion is used in a general sense of learning to solicit help, learning to depend upon others for making decisions or completing a task or judging a task and directing one in a task. Women it is thought, are often taught to depend upon others by being over-helped as children, by having their parents respond more quickly to their cries and preventing them from learning how to cope with frustration. But the 'learned helplessness' which has recently been associated with depression is far stronger, far more harmful to self-development than the social forms of help-seeking which women have been taught and which they can often use to their own ends. The particular form of learned helplessness which has now been linked to depression is learned not by social persuasion and example, but by frustration so cruel that we are taught to give up on ourselves as agents who can influence our lives. We learn helplessness not in the sense that we learn to ask for help but in the sense that we abandon all thoughts of help.

This phenomenon was discovered when a group of psychologists at the University of Pennsylvania were working on learning theories.[4] There are two phases in the experiment which exhibit learned helplessness. During the first phase an animal undergoes repeated electric shocks while harnessed, so that it is unable to move away from the area in which the shocks occur. During the second phase the shocks are repeated, but the animal is no longer harnessed. Normally a dog would immediately jump away from the unpleasant stimulus and find the part of the cage that is not electrified. The remarkable finding, however, was that a dog who had experienced repeated shocks while being harnessed did not move away from the electrified section of the cage, or in any other way try to prevent itself from receiving shocks even when it was longer harnessed. The animal shows no sign of its power to avoid pain. It does not complain, but passively accepts the traumatic shock. It can unlearn this helplessness only by being dragged to the safe part of the cage.

Before these experiments were linked to depression, the most widespread model of depression was that of anger turned inward. Depressed people seemed to be particularly unaggressive, and yet they were totally dissatisfied with everything and everyone around them, or crippled by envy – attitudes which were usually accompanied by hostility. In depression, then, it was thought that the expected anger was present, but turned upon oneself. Depression was seen as a statement of self-derision. Women were thought to be more prone to depression than men because women had good reason to be angry (at men, at the bias of society) yet were so thoroughly trained not to display anger that they had no choice but to bottle up anger and direct it upon themselves. It is a neat account, based on a popular version of Freud's theory of the mind, as a system of feelings which, unexpressed, become rabidly self-defeating. But this neat theory did not account for the central point of depression, which is the relentlessly negative view depressed people have of the world. Moreover, the particular type of negativism depressed people exhibited was similar to the 'giving up' of those tortured animals.

In experiments with people it was found that they responded as did the dogs. They were presented with noises they could not control and problems they could not solve, and then they seemed to accept the view of themselves as unable to control their environment or to understand it in a positive way, as an agent acting upon the environment. Even when they were subsequently presented with noises they could control and problems they would ordinarily be able to solve, they assumed they had no power, and refused to make any attempt to exercise their abilities. Moreover, learned helplessness in humans was characterised by passivity, reduced aggressiveness, diminished appetite – for food and sexual activity – sadness, anxiety, lowered self-esteem, decreased learning ability, as well as the chemical changes that are known to accompany depression.

Depression seems to grow out of the destructive ways people view their experiences. Depression occurs when a person suffers repeated failures in controlling the reinforcers of his or her environment – that is, he or she gets no satisfactory response from the significant people and institutions in his or her life. It occurs when there is insufficient reciprocity, or confirmation, or positive self-discovery. Needs and wishes appear futile. Failure is expected, and therefore when the depressed person fails, he or she does not adapt behaviour to the failure – for example, by changing tactics, strategies or goals. Learned helplessness generalises beyond the specific situation or situations in which it was originally learned. One does not conclude that there are simply certain areas in which one has no control, but rather that one is a person who is unable to control or influence anything. And it is not simply a state – like a state of shock. It is not something one can snap out of. It becomes a personality trait – one sees oneself as ineffectual and becomes an ineffectual person. Moreover, one blames oneself for one's failures and for one's troubles, and not only does one blame oneself but one explains the mistakes in terms of traits or qualities that are unchanging, rather than in terms of a single unfortunate choice or action. A depressed person will say, for example, that she did poorly on a test because she is not smart enough, rather than because she did not spend enough time revising, or that she lost a friend because she is not good at sustaining relationships rather than because she and her friend had specific differences. On the other hand, when depressed people experience good fortune, they tend to attribute it to luck, rather than to their own influence. When they successfully complete a task, they will claim that their success was due to the ease of the task, not to their skill. For bad fortune they look within themselves for the cause, and for good fortune they look to causes outside themselves. Thus they deprive themselves of a sense of success even when they do succeed: they allow failure to reinforce their depression.

The negative self-image involved in depression dominates everything else about depression. The sense of loss that may also characterise depression, therefore, is more a loss of a positive view of oneself, rather than a loss of a relationship. In fact, the depressed person may try to isolate herself because she has lost interest in other people, or lost her expectation that other people will reinforce her sense of self. The separations that often precede depression may be self-inflicted and a symptom, not a cause of depression. Women, like men, have strong affiliative needs – that is, needs for intimacy and growth with others – but it is not these needs that make them more prone to depression. Things can go wrong with relationships and lead to unhappiness, but unhappiness is not depression. Depression indicates a loss of power, and a giving up on regaining power. Current cures, which are proving more effective than antidepressant drugs, are based on the development of a sense of mastery. The therapy includes a series of graded tasks, which undercut the patient's negative views. A person who claims she cannot get out of bed will be instructed first to sit up, then to put her legs over the side, then told to take one step, then another. In this way the patient's view that she is helpless and weak is undercut.

Depression and Women

Depression is a woman's ailment because too often women neglect the importance of developing mastery. Because women are attuned to others' needs, they are apt to neglect their own. It is not a coincidence or contradiction that the so-called 'me' generation is interested not in immediate gratification and indulgence, but in working outside the home, and developing skills and interests which are related not to one's family, but to the professional world. The development of skills and the ability to function on one's own behalf in the professional world protect one from many misfortunes to oneself and to one's family. Marriages do not always last forever, nor does a husband's earning power. A woman who knows she will be helpless in certain circumstances – circumstances which can actually be expected to occur – will have a diminished view of her self. She may have been told she does not need to challenge the world outside her home. She may as a result have learned to fear to challenge it. And she may then come to believe that any challenge she made would be useless. She is then on the road to depression.

There would be little point to this book if I did not believe that women have a harder time of combining their various needs than do men. We all know how working fathers function, and we all know that very few mothers can function happily in the same way. Women do have specific needs to nurture their children. All too often the mothers' needs are read as the children's need for the mother, and that complicates things. Guilt overrides a mother's assessment of her own needs. But children are adaptable. They are not harmed by working mothers. We must believe this, because we need to work. Depression is a serious threat, and we must avoid it by learning mastery and facing stress – the good stress that goes along with challenge and self-expansion. We must be careful with ourselves, and carefully read our needs. We must learn to predict what our needs will be, and prevent ourselves from facing situations in which we cannot begin to meet them, situations in which we have learned to be helpless. Frustration and disappointment can become destructive. Our hopes can atrophy, as can our energies and abilities. For women there are few guidelines in meeting the needs of affiliation and the needs of self-expansion. Each woman must find her own way through the maze of compromises and conflicts, but she will not have the strength to do this if she does not recognise the breadth of her needs. Only if these different needs are acknowledged can we avoid the impasse of defeat before we start. The stupidity of that helplessness is learnt, and we must unlearn it, and remember to teach our children something different.

6
New Options – Having It All

The Successful Self-image

If any one person represents the new age of the professional woman, Emily James* does. Her skills and dedication, along with a doctorate in economics, earned her a responsible position in the International Monetary Fund in Washington. Her husband had an equally important position in the World Bank making them part of the 'new rich' in America – the people who have beaten the recession and inflation by amassing large joint incomes. Emily and her husband have two young children, and a good nanny to look after them. She embodies the ideal of having it all – husband, children and career. But gradually it became clear that something was going wrong, and that in the midst of enjoying what is thought to be a complete life, she was losing her self.

'I have a very clear self-image', she explained, 'I am independent. I do what I want – more or less. I am good at what I do. I make firm decisions, and I'm confident they are good decisions. But I've realised that my self-image is no longer valid.'

Her daughter was two and a half, and her son was one year old when she came to this conclusion. The children were making terrible scenes when she went to work, and if she had to go out again in the evening there was hell to pay. Even at this young age they were learning the meaning of time and knew the days of the week, because weekends meant there was time with mother. She saw her children growing and changing and suffering. It bothered her that she could be so distant from her children. She felt she did not understand them very well, and could not interpret their needs. It was an important objective of hers and her husband's that their children share their parents' values and enjoy their company. She believed, too, that timing was criticial. At five they would start school, and be away from home most of the day. If something was to be done, it had to be done now.

There are many women like Emily James today, women in their mid-thirties who learned to take advantage of career opportunities, women who had the self-confidence to learn the ropes of their professions so that they could be as effective as any man. As Emily says, 'You can have the best ideas in the world. You can be right every time. But unless you know how to present your ideas – when to send a memo, whom to send a memo to, when to make a phone call, and when to give up on an argument even when your point is good – you will end up wasting a lot of time, and you will get nowhere.' Women like Emily have learned to be political – not ruthless, not conniving, but well read in the rules of the game. They are not afraid of competing, and have a sense of themselves as fair in competition. They represent the best growth from the women's movement. They show independence and responsibility for their own lives and a new female self-respect. But this does not ensure a smooth combination of career and identity. We will take another look at Emily's story later.

Some of these women, like Barbara Thomas, a Commissioner in the Security and Exchange Control, and Carole

Bellows, former president of the Chicago Bar Association and partner in a large Chicago law firm, were raised with the idea that they would work. They never considered not having a career, and they were trained in a profession because they valued the security of having a specific qualification, one that had a good chance of offering security and luxury. These women who appear to be travelling a path they already know, one which will make them safe from the twists of fortune as a dependant upon a husband, none the less do not opt for mere safety, but tend to challenge new areas. When Barbara Thomas graduated from New York University Law School, second in a class of 323, she had many job offers, but firms always tried to steer her away from corporate law, which was the area of her choice. She prefers negotiation to litigation, for what might be considered 'female' reasons – she likes both parties to go away happy, rather than to see a win or lose situation, in which one party must have the worst – except that corporate law is more highly male dominated than any other law field. With characteristic firmness, she stood her ground and succeeded in corporate law; and like most women of this generation, the post-feminist generation, the generation growing up with feminist ideas and in a society already changing to accommodate such ideas, she has not suffered from her independence, but gained certainty and pride from it. She has not had to defend herself against the usual feminine feelings. She has not denied herself maternity, or denied the primacy of the maternal, as opposed to the paternal, bond. Her important life task now, with a young son, is to combine this independence and this bond. Her wishful fantasy is to have someone who will look after her, a personal secretary who will do her shopping, wash her hair, make social arrangements, write her thank you notes. She would like someone to look after her so that she could have time to look after the people who depend upon her. Since she does not have such a caretaker, she keeps anxiety at bay by making lists. Just to see that the tasks have some kind of order, and, perhaps, an end, however temporary, gives her a sense of greater control.

Independent – True or False?

These women breathe an independence that blessed their
lives and that creates unease in many other women.[6] Why
am I not like them?', a housewife may wonder. 'Why is
my life so unlike theirs? If only I had done this or that',
they may think, but the fact is they would have to be
different people to have done this or that. Independence
is not a quality everyone develops, though it is a quality
everyone needs. Women are often not encouraged to develop it as children, and this can be highly frustrating in
adult life. What is confusing, too, is the fact that many
young women have an appearance of independence and
adventurousness which is obviously false, because it
quickly comes to an end. We all know examples of
women who seem to guard their own interests closely. As
single women, or even as married women without children,
they appear quick to see their rights, and ready to hold
their ground. But marriage and motherhood can eclipse
that early promise so completely it might never have existed. I know that most women who value their careers fear
waywardness in themselves. Independence in women can be
undercut because women are so damnably responsive to
others' needs, especially to the needs of their children, and
because it is these needs above all others that are likely to
limit their professional ambitions. Their maternal commitments may be excessive because they want to protect their
husbands from the distractions and frustrations of combining career ambitions with parental responsibilities. Or, with
apparently no struggle at all, a woman may transfer her
ambitions to her family, and look for contentment and support from within her family. Suddenly her career, and the
independence linked to it, have diminished importance. Her
identity reverts to the traditional female pattern of identity
in relation to husband and children. She may believe she is
burdened by other responsibilities, but it is clear that she wel-
comes these responsibilities, as though she has secretly been
waiting to ease the burden of independence for which she was
not fully prepared. She may feel closer to her mother now,

because she sees herself in the traditional female image. The sense of homecoming, in giving up her career-oriented identity, makes it seem right, or inevitable; and we sometimes feel, when looking at such a person's history, that the early independence was a game played for the fun and glamour of it, and that the stress of independence – the stress which comes when we have to refuse others' requests and remind them that they must check their expectations of us – had not been acknowledged. The multitude of such cases remind us that women often have poor training in independence and self-assertion.

Yet in other women – and it is very difficult to point to general differences in their backgrounds or training, I can only point to the different ways they solve problems as they arise – the youthful independence shows a lifelong characteristic. It will be guarded, preserved and valued. It may be done so quietly, without feminist fanfare, and yet it will be more effective than almost anything else in supporting the feminist aim.

Emily James never deliberately planned a career, yet all her decisions, as a teenager and young adult, indicate an instinctive desire to create and preserve an adult independence. She grew up in a small midwestern town in the US. She admired her father and thought him exceptionally intelligent and successful (though her view of his achievements now is more moderate, and she hopes to surpass him), and though she took her mother for granted when she was growing up, she now appreciates her, and sees her as a stable force in the family. She values the certainty that reigned in her family, and the clear sense of right and wrong. Like many successful young women I interviewed, Emily was attached to both her parents, and admired both of them. It is often thought that the successful woman is more attached to her father (this was the case with the managerial business women who were born in the first part of the century) and that the woman who clings to independence, as opposed to the woman whose youthful display of independence is merely play, rejects her mother's domesticity, and associates dependency needs with weakness, tending to deny them in herself because they belong to the 'despised self'. But these new young professional women, who combine family and career, seldom spurn their mother's homemaking, and usually feel they benefited from having their mother at home.

The greatest conflict Emily had with her parents was just before she went to university. As she says, she 'should have gone a year earlier'. This is a mild description of her obvious desperation. She finished high school early, without telling her parents, and took a job as a secretary, learning how to type along the way. It was a boring job, but it allowed her to move away from home and establish a life of her own. She went to the state university (which was all her family could afford) at the appointed time. She did well, and upon graduation, obtained a teaching fellowship at Berkeley. Even during these years, when her dissatisfactions with her family and herself were rampant, she displayed a level-headed ability to get what she wanted. She did not bargain for a false independence, as so many young women do, by getting married. She did not spend her university years enjoying freedom in the form of futile rebellion. Always, she had a 'nose' for her best adult interests. When she completed her doctorate at Berkeley she was still engaged to a hometown boy, whom she loved. She had a choice between a job in Chicago and a job in Washington. She was tempted to choose the Chicago job, since it was closer to her fiancé, who was studying law at the University of Chicago, but at the last minute, on a 'whim', she chose the Washington position. Washington was a city she did not know, and it seemed more exciting to her. The date for the marriage was still set, but as it grew nearer she began to feel more and more distressed about it. She could see her future clearly. Her husband, once he was qualified as a lawyer, would join his father's firm. They would be a prominent couple in the city, but it was a small city, and there would be few opportunities for her. She might have had some kind of a career – the present wife of her former fiancé is a teacher – but she could not have stretched herself as she wanted. The marriage that to some would have seemed inevitable and necessary, came to appear impossible.

Many of the women I interviewed mentioned engagements which did not materialise. These are common enough phenomena, but in many cases they could be recognised as attempts to visualise different possible futures. These unfulfilled engagements were most common among women who did not have a clear idea of their career. They were very uncommon among women who had decided upon a profession early in life and who had geared their education accordingly. The women who had a strong desire for independence but an as yet vague notion of their adult working lives, used various engagements to explore not their feelings for a person but their self-identity.

Sally Quinn, a journalist and novelist, now married to the editor of the *Washington Post,* referred casually to several engagements which caused her to move from one city to another and one job to another. She was in fact not so much following fiancés as gaining new job experience, and looking for a role that suited her, after she had decided that her initial ambition to become an actress would not be realised. She did not marry Ben Bradlee – and this was her first marriage – until she was thirty-eight, and it was through her association with him that she consolidated her writing career.

Life Patterns

It has been found that women typically do not have as clear a life pattern as do men, that women do not like the typical male, spend their adolescence developing a life dream and plans for fulfilment, but rather retain a pliancy in self-development because they develop in tandem with a mate, and pause in self-development until they find a mate.[1] Whereas a man would choose his mate in accordance with his dream – choosing a woman who would support him in his hopes and trials, who would go well with his achievements, and who would enforce his sense of what he wanted to be – a woman would choose her mate and then mould her dream to his.[2] This was not true of women who had already achieved a sense of their adult self, however. These false engagements did display some lack of self-definition, but they were false engagements because the women rejected the notion of defining themselves according to another's adult plans. These women, when they did choose husbands, chose carefully. They chose husbands who would accept their way of life and the limited domestic services thereby implied.

Independence and Attachment

It strikes many people as odd that the heroes and heroines in Victorian novels are outlandishly young. When they are making decisions which set the course of their lives, resisting or succumbing to various temptations, judging or failing to judge characters who will offer them fulfilment or frustration, they are usually around nineteen or twenty. This was due partly to the convention of having many stories end with marriage, since marriage then was considered more permanent than it is today, but it is true that when we are emerging from adolescence we have the highly important task of carving out our adult reality. Failure to make use of our new independence and failure to honour our needs as adults may set us back and confuse us miserably. Decisions are not irreversible, and there is always time to repair damage or to correct wrong turnings, but our chances are not endless. Abilities and interests can atrophy. We can quickly lose self-confidence, and the youthful expansive vision. And the attachments we form in these early years complicate any changes in our lives we may want to make later. When older characters change they may, for this reason, suffer and inflict suffering on others, so that an impossible dilemma arises between their new awareness and their established attachments. Nora in Ibsen's *A Doll's House* realises how her humanity has been undercut first in her father's house, where she was his plaything, and then in her 'own' home, when she was her husband's plaything. She sees how she has been functioning only as an accessory to the men's domestic convenience and hypocritical morality. Seeing this she leaves, to get to know herself and to find a better way to live. Bravo! But the question of her three children is more than niggling. Ibsen knew this. He could not envisage a future for her, having abandoned her children, and so a shot rings out after she shuts the door of the home behind her.

Neglect of the past and of the concreteness of attachments made in the past, even when these attachments have been formed through mistaken decisions and unwise commitments, is what makes Gail Sheehy's studies of adults' 'passages' so shallow. The future is not a clean slate. The exhilaration of thinking it is, is often manic. We are bound by what we are, and what we have let ourselves become. Once we have developed certain false dependencies it is very difficult to allow different needs to find expression. Many women who have come to feel lost and cheated in their lives cannot understand where they went wrong. They envy professional women who stood out against a 'secure' marriage and who had a much broader or deeper sense of that youthful freedom. They do not understand why their opportunities came to an end, or when they ended. Looking back, it always seems as though they ended long before marriage, and before motherhood. They ended with a lack of determination, and a lack of vision. But this deficiency is so difficult to detect, because many women are free of it without appearing to be consciously firm of will, or without having a specific goal in sight. Sometimes an unexpected success will put them on the right road. Margaret Drabble's first novel was published when she was having her first baby, and only its favourable reception made her realise where her talent, and her career, lay. Sometimes a mentor will put one straight – but a person has luck like this only when considerable effort has already been expended and considerable achievement proved. Women have had a more difficult time in developing those skills that will lead to success and independence because they have not been taught their value. Even women who believe they know their value have fallen far short of their own ideals, and been sidetracked, and only those who are blessed with an inner direction come out ahead — ahead of the overdevelopment of dependency needs, which may lock them in that attachment to their children which is so difficult to break because it contains so much that is real and true.

Maternal Harassment

Emily James is among a group of new women who strike an excellent balance in their needs, who have been, sometimes unconsciously but always with subtlety, finely attuned to their needs and interests without being unfair to others. She is happily married to a man she chose in part because he did not think his masculinity was undermined in joining her as an equal partner in care for the home and the children. She is not out to prove anything, to herself or to other women, by trying to be a superwoman — as the feminists of ten years ago often did. Emily agrees that she has been lucky, that the path for her ambitions was paved in the 1970s, and that the viability of her life as mother and professional has been confirmed, and is being confirmed, by many others. She does not have to bear the pioneer's burden of abrasive self-consciousness. She agrees that she is lucky, but she also expects to be lucky, and this expectation gives her confidence. But now, even as she can be seen to 'have it all', she is facing problems which will affect her life-style. When I first interviewed her she said,

> I do see myself as competent and independent and able to do a good job. I know I can find efficient ways of doing things, and that when they are done I can be satisfied. But I've noticed something is changing. My daughter wants me to take her ice-skating, and I can't, because at the weekend I have to catch up with too many other things. I care terribly about my children, and I expect to do well by them. But I don't seem to be doing a very good job as a mother at the moment. I feel harassed — and that's not me.

I laughed outright. Did she really think she could have it all – her career, her two children, a well-run home – without being harassed? Most of the women who do 'have it all' accept being torn between two sets of needs, and two sets of responsibilities. They take the plunge anyway, and view guilt or self dissatisfaction with a humorous distance, as though to say, 'Well, guilt comes with it. I'm not going to feel like a good mother, but I suppose my children will be all right in the end.' It was clear how harassed most women were simply in making appointments for the interviews. Barbara Thomas had to cancel our first appointment because she had to fly back to New York when her infant son became ill. Donna Karan, Anne Klein's successor at the New York designer firm Anne Klein & Co., had to cancel our appointment because she had to take her daughter to summer camp. There was no room to fit in anything extra, and I therefore agreed to interview working mothers where they were not working – that is, when they were working only as mothers. There were times when this made me lapse into a role as mere observer, while the women attended to other things. Ann Compton, from the American Broadcasting Company, suggested we meet on a Saturday, but it turned out that on alternate Saturdays she is responsible for White House coverage, and shares child care with her husband. Often she takes her oldest son with her to the White House – for on Saturdays things are usually slow, and she expects to be finished by noon. The day we met she had to cover the President's regular Saturday radio address, which seldom makes news, but the networks cover it all the same. This particular morning, however, heralded the news of the Lebanon massacre, and if the President were to use the broadcast to make a statement, it would be prime news. In preparation, therefore, Ann had to make a lot of contacts, find out what she should be prepared to ask, what line to expect the President to take, and what the various implications might be. While she was doing this she was also getting her children's breakfast. Then she collected along with her papers, a bag of toys to entertain her son. Once in her office in the White House she had to take him to the toilet, even though he had protested, when passing it on their way to the office, that he did not need to use it. He then complained that he was thirsty. She poured him some milk while she spoke on the telephone, and he promptly spilled it. Well, a three-year-old is no fool. He knows how to punish his mother for inattentiveness. There is no point in raging against his staunch self-centredness. He will simply retaliate in one way or another. There is no point in trying to explain the importance of what she is doing. She heard that the President would not make a statement on the radio broadcast, but might make one later in the day, and she realised she might have to spend the afternoon in the White House – yet she had promised to take her son to a birthday party at noon! Her husband, who had also been working that morning and had had the charge of their younger son, could not be reached by telephone. Apparently he had already left his office for the party. She was told that the wording of the statement was being changed. Guessing that this would take several hours, she decided to risk nipping off to deliver her son to the party, but just as she was leading him down the driveway she heard that the President was about to hold an impromptu press conference. I had been tagging along, sharing awkward smiles meant to convey sympathy. When she turned to me I knew exactly what she wanted. 'I'll take him', I offered and her body sagged with relief. She did not, after all, have to ruin her son's day in order to do her job.

These antics are all too familiar to a working mother. The roles of a nanny or child-minder or nurse become crucial, but these do not function full time as do children. 'Brooding time' – the freedom to muse about one's work, to let one's mind go blank, anticipating and then developing ideas – is what many women found they lacked, and for some it was crippling. One writer gave up the more creative side of her work after her third child was born because she discovered that when she was faced with a blank sheet of paper all she could write was a shopping list. The professional woman who has the luxury of being a mother and a full-time worker has to function with efficiency and single-

mindedness, and has to ignore that awful, heart-rending
pressure from one's children.

Harassed? Was Emily James not thoroughly naïve to be
surprised at being harassed, and to refuse to tolerate it?
How could she suppose she would feel she was giving her
children her best, while she gave that to her career, too?
But this naïvety served her well, for she was able, for a
considerable time, to avoid harassment. She had the good
(and rare) fortune to have an excellent nanny. Most women
had trouble finding a good nanny. Most had to look abroad
for one. In America, English-speaking nannies were expensive gems. A female colleague of Emily's said that she
had advertised in the *Washington Post,* had had a hundred
replies, and not one was suitable. Emily's husband had
found her a marvellous New Zealand nanny – who now
works for Sally Quinn and Ben Bradlee; these gems are
preserved by the elite. Emily was protected from a sense of
being harassed, too, because her husband did take a full
share – that is, 50 per cent – in domestic responsibilities
– and this is still highly unusual; but it did not protect
Emily from feeling the pressure of her role as the primary
parent, because her children showed a marked preference
and need for her.

Is Harassment Destiny?

If women can 'have it all', why should they have to lose a
sense of doing it all properly? If they are to have it all, and
do it all, then they must learn to delegate – as in fact
Emily had done when her children were infants. It was the
nanny who knew when they needed new shoes, and who
went out to buy them. It was the nanny who looked out for
earaches, and who knew when the next tetanus shot was
due. The nanny decided when to put the babies onto solid
food, and when to toilet train them. It was a Victorian style
of delegation that is very rare today. Most women are jealous of their privileged position as mother, and even though
they may consult experts, they believe that in the end, they
know best, or at least want to have primary involvement in

the ordinary health care of their children. Many agreements between father and mother about delegation of responsibilities are half-hearted on both sides, because the father is unsure how to do things, and because the mother prevents him from learning because she wants to do things herself. Many complaints against a father's ineptness or reluctance to help are devious means of bragging about one's proficiency as a mother. It is hard to share responsibility for the children, but Emily did manage to do it, until her children singled her out and spoke of their need for her. But if she was sensitive to these demands, was she not also sensitive to the bonding that must have taken place during her three months of maternity leave?

'I was ready to go back to work', she replied.

Subsequently I discovered that this was an understatement. She was desperate to get back to work. Nor had she actually taken a full maternity leave, for she had continued to give evening lectures, write papers and arrange lunch-time conferences throughout those three months.

Many women were unexpectedly seduced by their infants, and did find their priorities changed as they looked after them. Some dreaded returning to work, and losing that continuous contact with their child, which, especially in the beginning of the child's life, can be not merely satisfying but intoxicating. Even these women, however, did return to work, though some changed their long-term goals, hoping to spend more time with their children in the future, or gradually compiling reasons to stop work after they had a second child. Those mothers who were faced with health problems, however, had an extra drain put upon them, and the seduction was mixed with poison. 'Having a baby was the best thing that has ever happened to me', Sally Quinn said, whose son had open heart surgery at five months' old, and who has been frequently ill since, 'and his illness is the worst.' She extended her leave from the *Washington Post* after his birth, and continued to work on her novel, which she eventually finished, though she calculated that it had taken a year longer to write because of his illness. This had made her redefine her future goals, too. 'I suppose I did not wait until I was forty-one to have a child only to work full time', she said, and believes that she will work only part time for the next five years.

The Baby Grenade

Having a child can change the marriage, too, creating unexpected problems. Nora Ephron, the New York journalist, whose marital despair was widely publicised in her novel *Heartburn*, describes the birth of a child as a grenade thrown into a marriage. The husband's feelings for the wife can change dramatically. He may now identify her with his mother, and find sexual feelings towards her forbidden. He may feel romance threatened, or be jealous of her involvement with the child and seek revenge or consolation in the arms of another woman. This seldom alienates the mother from her child, but rather changes her options so that she has to think in terms both of child and work. Independence may be forced upon her. But it is also possible that she may be forced to become independent as a parent. She may have expected help with the parenting of her child, and the father may have agreed to that, but she finds instead that the father does not prove good at parenting, or that he falls back upon earlier expectations and allows the mother to carry the entire burden. 'When I was a baby, my father was away for years. It was during the war', one husband explained to his wife, who complained that the preparental agreement he had made about sharing child responsibility was not being carried out. He meant to say that the child would be all right – after all he had survived – but what he was actually saying was that he was as he was because he had been deprived of a father as an infant. He had had no training as a father – how could his wife therefore expect him to be active as a father?

Along with the changes that may take place around her, the mother faces threats from within. 'I still want to compose', Elizabeth Lutyens reported crying as her first born emerged from her body. It was the cry of a woman whose expansive identity was under threat. Child-bearing is said to be creative, and it would, she feared, sap her need to compose music. Motherhood can overpower one, and make one's need to nurture, and the sense of one's connection to others, and one's responsiveness to others' needs, eclipse one's need for autonomy and challenge. Many women also fear the drain on their energy, the practical difficulties that will make other work and other interests so much more difficult to enjoy. Many women display a manic energy and determination after the birth of their first child as they show they are not cast in the role of the traditional mother, who has no interests outside her home and her child. Many of these women see for the first time that their independence is under threat, that a new, overriding claim is made upon them which nothing, short of insanity, can deny. They are very keen to reestablish a connection with their former lives, a connection which may now seem tenuous. Moreover, they still have the needs which led to their former interests. They do not become totally different people, but they are inevitably changed, and are unsure precisely how they are changed, or what the implications of the change are. Some women protect themselves by adopting a cool attitude towards the helpless infant. This is what Emily James did. 'I'm not particularly interested in babies', she said. 'They're not quite human beings.'

Many other mothers respond this way. Such a response often leads to postpartum depression, because the new mother is in close contact with notions of what a mother should feel and simultaneously isolated from them by her own lack of feeling. It often takes time – sometimes several months – for a woman to feel attached to her infant, and some mothers are naturally more 'maternal' than others. The problem of one's own feelings towards a child remains something of a forbidden subject, especially when those feelings are simply low key. Strong negative feelings are now more easily acknowledged than simple coolness. But such coolness can be a good defence against the overpowering changes in our lives that are bound to take place when we become mothers, especially if we do not worry about our feelings, but have sufficient faith in our ability to meet and recognise responsibilities, regardless of how we feel. Emily was able to use that initial distance from her child to good effect, but like many women who manage to continue with their career, and to continue to commit themselves to their careers after the birth of a child, she complicated her life by being taken in (for a short time, but for long enough) by the superwoman image. She was coping well with a child. Her life was well paced. She had a reliable nanny and a helpful husband. Though she had never planned having any children (her husband, who wanted them, agreed when they married that she need not have them, that though he would like children, this desire was not central to his life) she had felt that putting off the decision whether to have children was becoming, as she approached thirty, a decision not to have children, and this was not a decision she was happy with. Having had one child, she believed she should have another, and having coped so well with one, she felt she could cope with another. Her husband believed it was too soon, but he none the less agreed. There was, after all, the bonus of getting the hectic early years over soon. But her second child was more demanding than the first. One of her brothers was having some personal problems, and she wanted time to spend with him. She had recently changed departments in the Fund, and she wanted time to become adept at her new position. The stress took her by surprise. She found she could not do everything at once, and yet there was nothing that seemed less important than anything else. With characteristic clear-sightedness she knew something had to change. She would not accept this rift between her desire to be competent, thorough and reliable, and her abilities within the given circumstances.

But what were her alternatives? If she cut down on her duties at work, she would be doing a completely different kind of job, with greatly diminished influence. She would not be called upon for certain professional tasks if she was known to keep rigid hours, if she was known to do less than her best possible work. It would be better simply to take extended leave and be out of the picture for a while, but leave untarnished her current reputation. But how could she give up work? She was perhaps ready for a change from the Fund. She had been there for seven years, but did not want to stay there forever, and if she was going to change jobs, she should do it soon, before she became entrenched in the Fund's hierarchy. So she could resign, and then at some later date start again. But in the meantime, could she simply stay at home with the children? She knew from the experience of two maternity leaves that staying at home with the children, while her husband went out to work, was simply not viable for her. She felt the mounting demands of her two young children and wanted to meet them, but she could not meet them as an ordinary housewife.

Whose Problem Is It?

Dr David Scarff, a leading child psychologist in Washington DC, claims that a woman who is unhappy at home with her child all day, has a problem. It is a problem for the mother because then she is unhappy doing what is best for the child. But children are adaptable. They need human beings for parents, and human beings differ in their approach to parenting. A woman who is unhappy at home all day with the children – and most women are – has a problem because it is not at all clear how she can reorganise her life to accommodate needs, which are sometimes pressing – as they had become in Emily's case – to be with one's children without being isolated as a housewife. The problem demands a creative solution, and it requires cooperation. Emily did not want to trade in the stress of a working mother for the stress and frustration of a housewife. She and her husband came to an agreement – they would both give up their jobs for two years to be with their children.

It was a decision which amazed their colleagues. Give up two splendid jobs during a recession? Accept a drastic cut in income? Use all one's savings to travel for two years? It was a risk many could not imagine taking, but Emily's confidence made her deny that the risk was great. She believed that the risk was not that they would be without jobs, and without an income, but that one or the other of them would

be forced, for a while, to take a less than fully satisfactory
job. She and her husband had deliberately chosen a fairly
risky investment strategy, on the ground that as young
working people they could afford to risk the savings portion
of their incomes in the hopes of a high return. Their financial good luck, which arose from good sense, gave them the
privilege of taking this side-step so many working mothers
dream of.

Most working mothers live with a sense that they are
cheating someone – either themselves, since they are deprived of time to follow those personal interests that are
unrelated to either the career or the home, or their colleagues, or their husbands, or their children. These women
feel guilty, for example, because their child, who is at a
nursery or day-care centre, picks up colds and flus from the
other children. They feel guilty because they have to leave a
meeting early to be home when the nanny goes off duty.
They feel guilty because their children want more time with
them, or because their husbands or boyfriends want more
time with them, or because they themselves want more time
with those they love. Working mothers learn to live with
guilt. Most of them accept it, somewhat humorously, as inevitable. But we need women who refuse to think it inevitable. Many women who were Emily's age spoke of wanting
a change, of planning to seek a change, so that they could
find a new balance between their work and their children,
but as far as I know, Emily was the only one who persisted,
and carried out her plans – but then she did have remarkable cooperation from her husband.

So for two years, Emily and her husband shared their
lives with their children. They skied, they hiked, they
camped, and they found they could accept a different pace.
Emily now believes that in terms of learning to be a
mother, the break was a full success. 'I have had my share
of both the ups and downs', she reported, 'and I both love
and understand my children more as people in their own
right.' But she did not actually stop working during that
period. She continued to act as a consultant for the Fund,
and this involved not only time alone in her study but

travels away from her family. However much she values her attachment to her children, she clearly could not function as a full-time mother. She is too fully attuned to her expansive needs to see any point in denying them. She plans to return to a fairly structured career path, yet she is no longer in such a hurry to reach the top. On returning to Washington she saw her colleagues' devotion to their jobs as 'brittle', and she now feels an aversion to reentering that particular rat race. She hopes to find other companies, or other places, where it is possible to strike a better balance.

This brave and sensible vision acknowledges the new split in women's life patterns, which is now very marked in America. More and more women are growing up with the idea that they will work, but when they work, they find that, as mothers, certain traditional feelings will not disappear. The contemporary American novel simplifies this. Its new subject is that of a high-powered woman who becomes a mother, discovers her maternal strengths, and eschews her previous ambitions (as in Freda Bright's *Futures* and Ann Berk's *Fast Forward*). The true picture, however, is much less easily resolved. Women as mothers do discover maternal passions and an overwhelming responsiveness to their children's wishes (which they usually perceive as needs) but they retain their expansive needs. Previous ambitions do not lose meaning, nor do determined personalities suddenly change. Women in this position do 'have it all'. They have their children, and they have their careers. They usually keep both. The cost is simply a reasonable way of life.

7
The Wage Learners: Working as Necessity

Many women resist going back to work after the birth of their children because they don't want to miss out on that first smile, the first word, the first step. Other women dread the prospect of a child seeking comfort from his minder, rather than from the mother. Others believe that only they can give the child the best a child can have, not because they are supreme in the art of child-minding but because they have a supreme relation to their child. Our children have only one infancy, and one childhood, and women have to weigh up their various needs. Always there are trade-offs, and the best we can hope for is to survive our decisions. But for some women, choice, and the anxiety and guilt that accompany it, appear as luxuries.

Mothers Have to Work

In the United States over half the women of working age do in fact work, and of the women who work, more than a quarter are head of the household, responsible for supporting themselves and at least one dependant. Of the women who work, over a third have children under the age of eighteen, and almost a quarter of working women have children under the age of four. Among married couples, where both husband and wife work, many could not meet their fixed monthly debt obligations without substantial contributions from the wife's salary. In Britain the percentage of working mothers is roughly the same, and in fact more women are going back to work after having a family than in any other Western European country. In both countries, too, over a third of the women who marry will be divorced and self-supporting by the time they are thirty-five. In Britain new bills are pending which will require divorced women to support themselves, and even as the law now stands, many women are forced to support themselves and their dependants because alimony or child support payments cannot be enforced. Only 12 per cent of newly divorced mothers live solely on maintenance, and after ten years of divorce only 6 per cent rely on payments by their ex-husbands as their main source of income. Mothers work because they have to. And in many cases, the pressure to support oneself and one's children goes hand in hand with being a single parent. So women who have to work are also women who have the greatest responsibilities as mothers.

Many women who have to work discover this necessity suddenly. They may be totally unprepared, having planned their lives as a dependant. They saw their role as mother and homemaker – necessary jobs which generate no income. The world of work is not really 'out there', separate from their world, but it seems so, and it therefore becomes so. They have to learn new rules, new ways of presenting themselves, they have to discover marketable skills, and develop those skills. Many women who face the necessity of wage-earning for the first time may be trapped into low-paying jobs which have no promotion or training opportunities, simply because they are glad to get whatever job they can. Even a woman in her late twenties may feel old, or actually be old in terms of job training. It is difficult to overestimate the speed with which a woman who has had a family but no career, can see her career prospects disintegrate. She loses confidence, she loses guts, she loses the will to make her life better. In her fear, she is glad just to survive.

Colette Dowling, author of *The Cinderella Complex*, described how she nursed an alcoholic husband, and after she finally divorced him, how she supported herself and her three children as a freelance journalist in New York. When she remarried, she found that she was turning to domestic occupations, decorating rooms and making jam rather than continuing to complete work projects and seek new projects. She was, in her eyes, committing woman's sin against herself. She was becoming nothing more than a homemaker and mother. She was giving into her dependency needs, thus both demeaning herself and putting herself at risk. Well, taking a little break after all those years of stress and pressure does not really seem like the self-sabotage Dowling makes it out to be. She slights the value and purpose, the possibility of fulfilment, in domesticity. Because these skills are unmarketable, she assumes they are worthless. She is the most recent in a long line of feminists who simply do not see that women are doing something real, something both purposeful and satisfying, something even essential, when they mother. But her hard-core message, though grim, is a valid one: women are likely to be forced to be self-supporting; therefore they would be well advised to plan their lives with this necessity in mind. Because they are likely to be self-supporting at some time, they should always be prepared to be self-supporting, and the only way one can ensure one's earning power, is to be an earner now.

It is a good message, if you value safety above all else – not that this policy ensures a future income. Women, like men, can become redundant. Skills developed in one workplace can cease to have any marketable use. But it is about the best bet we can make. Our children have two parents, and we should be able to count on this, but we cannot. Fathers cannot count on their children always having a mother, either, but they are usually sufficiently well-positioned to employ someone to look after their children, or to endure the hassle of looking after them more or less while they work because they will be content to make do as a child-raiser, in much the same way many women will be content to make do with a low-paying job. Anything a father does will be seen as good enough. He will not have the guilt that a working mother is bound to have. He will not share the mother's expectations as a parent. Dowling does not consider the woman's conflict. Her attitude is that women must snap out of their dependency. She does not consider the fact that their attachment to their children, not laziness, not weakness, is often the cause of financial dependence.

Can Women Ever Work Like Men?

Women are not just like men, and if working mothers became just like working fathers, they would be killing an important and valuable part of themselves. It is not surprising then that the mothers I met who were forced to work as men, in that they suddenly faced the financial responsibilities men expect to face, developed a distinct female independence. Many men who work so hard that they are virtually cut off from their families claim that they are none the less working for their families. This is not true. They may indeed be pleased to see their families enjoying the fruits of their labour, but their careers are bound up with their identities, and provide a focus of direction and meaning. Nor do women, who are forced to work for themselves and their families, and who in the process develop a demanding career, work only for their families, but they are more aware of the role their family's well-being plays in self-satisfaction. There is a special pride in succeeding in a man's world and in fulfilling a 'man's' obligations, just as there is a special fear in facing those obligations. But even while a mother forced to work looks at her work as being done for her children, she knows that it threatens to take something away from them – herself. The relation between a mother who is forced to work, and who is a single parent, and her children as they gradually come to realise the mother's needs, is remarkable. The mother seeks means of enforcing her maternal position, with its privileges and strains, and the more successful she is in her career the better able she is to do this – a balance which is certainly not found with any regularity in the case of successful men.

Repeatedly I found that the pressures upon mothers who worked because they simply had to work, enforced their maternal identity, allowing them to overcome terrific odds against being successful either as mothers or as professional people. Valerie Wade, who now, at sixty, owns her own multimillion-dollar real estate business in Florida, was most unpromising mother material. As a child, Valerie was boarded out – an archaic, illegal practice whereby the mother who does not wish to care for her child herself, but who has some money, pays another couple to take the child into their home. It is like a private method of fostering, but without the controls and support offered to legal foster parents. And, when parents do resort to this practice, they usually have less than a healthy concern for their child, and do little to see that the care, once the child is out of their hands, is satisfactory. The first family Valerie stayed with, when she was four months old, was contacted through a woman her mother happened to meet on a train. The woman's brother had recently married but his wife could not have children, though she wanted them. Some financial arrangement was made – Valerie thinks her mother paid them about ten dollars a month – and thus began a series of 'homes' wherein she suffered the strictness of those who want to keep children out of the way, the neglect of those who expect children to be no bother (she still bears the ill effects of a broken elbow that was never set), and the sexual abuse of those who have no respect for children. Her mother visited her from time to time – Valerie thinks it was about twice a year – and those occasions were like visits from the Queen. She lived for them. She dreamt about them. Her fondest hope was to gain her mother's love, but of course she never did. Her father, she believes,

108

did love her, but he was weak, and succumbed to the regal charm of his wife. As in Hansel and Gretel, he allowed the woman to disown the children. But the father died when she was eleven, and he never had the strength to save her.

Maternal deprivation is often cyclical. The mother who rejects her children, or is unable to care for them, is often a woman who as a child was neglected, or uncared for, or cared for in institutions. It is difficult to see how Valerie could have received the good-enough mothering that produces not only a nonpsychotic adult, but one capable of caring for her own children. And the beginning of her adult history was highly unfavourable, because that began when she was really a child. Having no parents to care for her, and no home of her own, she married at fourteen (by lying about her age) and had her first child when she was sixteen. By the time she was eighteen she had two children, and she was a widow. This was the perfect set-up for a rejecting mother. How could she be expected to cope? They had had no insurance – eighteen-year-olds do not take out insurance. She had no job, no training, no support from her own family. Her mother was not interested in hearing about the daughter's plight. It was probably trumped up anyway, like those 'exaggerated' reports of sexual harassment. The daughter just wanted to lift a few dollars off her.

But there are miracles of resilience. What sometimes becomes an excuse for retaliation can also become a means of reparation. A child left with two babies, a child with little training for motherhood, became a woman determined to protect her own children from the life she had had. And she knew something that many working mothers do not know. She knew that whatever her children had to go through because she had to work, would not be as awful as what she had gone through in being separated from her mother and in being denied her mother's love. Her children had to be in another's care throughout the day, but they would remain with her, aware of her concern and love, and they would therefore survive.

The Advantages of Being a Female Breadwinner

Women who work because they must work have some advantage over those mothers who know they work primarily to fulfil their own needs. They have good reason to believe that their children are better off because they work, and that therefore any drawbacks from working appear as part of the given set-up, rather than as something the mother is gratuitously inflicting upon the children. Mothers whose work is a necessity do not avoid guilt completely, but there is less anxiety attached to the guilt, for the guilt is more like regret about how things are than a measure of one's selfishness. Guilt remains because mothers simply do feel responsible for anything that goes wrong with their children, any pain they suffer, any accidents which occur, any neglect the children feel they have endured, however unreasonable the children's feelings may be – and children do tend to be unreasonable. The mother's guilt is part of the fantasy that she has control over her children's lives. It is not so much a symptom of megalomania but of that gigantic vulnerability that strikes a mother in regard to her children.

The way the sense of responsibility extends beyond reason can be seen in parents' attitudes towards handicapped children. Beverley Sills, the soprano and current director of the New York City Opera, has two handicapped children, one of whom is not only deaf but severely autistic, and she claims that nothing can undermine a mother's confidence as much as a handicapped child. A mother is much less likely to return to work after having a handicapped child because she feels she must learn everything about helping the child, and give everything to the child, sometimes in an attempt to limit herself as the child is limited, but often with the more positive goal of helping the child make the best of his abilities. It can be the self-defeating task Margaret Drabble describes in her novel *The Ice Age,* which concludes by saying the 'enlightened' mother of a child with Down's Syndrome faces a blank and hopeless future, but people are not so cut and dried, even when they take time off from their expansive interests. The birth of a handicapped child is such a blow to a mother that there will, inevitably, be a time of remapping one's priorities. In the end Beverley Sills not only returned to work, but returned to a brilliant and demanding career, and she tried to wean herself away from guilt by learning about birth defects and joining a group which helps parents to overcome the same shock and humiliation and sense of uselessness she suffered.

Even healthy, normal children never, to their mothers, seem safe enough. Mothers who protect children too much put them in other kinds of danger, of which they have become all too aware during the past fifteen years. Women know how ridiculous they can be as mothers, and they are caught in a bind between their own feelings for their children, and their knowledge that their children need some reprieve from the natural intensity of mother love; and they are caught between the power of their love and sense of responsibility, and their own need for fulfilment. It is a highly delicate balance that is necessary to make things work. Neglect of children does not work, and overprotection does not work. Maternal guilt is strange in its helplessness. Usually guilt involves some sense of foreknowledge – that one had reason to know one's actions would be harmful. Maternal guilt lies outside the bounds of normal culpability. A mother is aware of many choices, and knows that she cannot predict the effects of her decisions. A mother whose choices are more limited may come out of the decision-making process a little ahead.

Valerie, at eighteen, had to find some set-up that worked. It merely had to hold together – that was all she could hope for. It was not a question of doing the best possible, it was a question of coping. She had a friend who was divorced and who had one son. The friend lived with her mother, who worked at night – from eight to midnight. Valerie got a job as a salesgirl and moved in with her friend. The young women worked during the day, while the mother (who slept from midnight to eight) looked after the children, and went out to work herself when the two mothers came home. It was in many ways a cosy arrangement, but it required the cooperation of three people whose schedules would have to remain fixed. It was the set-up for a low-key, low-paying job, for a woman who just wanted to make do – perhaps until she married again. But Valerie's youth and ignorance actually functioned on her behalf. She had heard of people making it in the big city (she was a fan of radio soap operas) and she thought she could, too. After a year she had saved a little money, and she left the small Ohio town where she had been living, to try her luck in New York. This was just after the war, and there were many young women sharing her optimism for a new life, many of whom had lost boyfriends or husbands. She looked in the newspaper for a flat to share, found a job at B. Altman's (a large New York department store) and a day-care centre for her children, one subsidised for children of soldiers. (Her husband had not been killed in action, but he had been in the army.) Her first task at work was to plead for Saturdays off so that she could spend it with her children. She explained that this was unheard of in a retail store, which tends to be busiest on Saturdays. Salespeople will take a day off during the week, and work on Saturday. She is very proud of the fact that she had the guts to ask, and the stature to get, her Saturdays off work.

Success often stimulates other success, and increases one's expectations. Valerie's life at this stage might not have appeared successful to many women, but it was to her – because she was managing to keep her children and to care for them. This might have been mere drudgery to someone else, but to Valerie it was a remarkable feat because she could not take it for granted. And because she thought of herself as being successful she moved forward in her work, whereas most of her friends remained as salesgirls. She soon became a buyer – that is, choosing which items the store would purchase rather than simply selling what had been chosen. When she was in her mid-twenties she married again. Any tendency she had to be taken care of by a man was surely tested here. Her husband was a wealthy and prominent professional man, and about forty years old. He was generous with the children in terms of giving them presents, but Valerie describes him as being selfish with himself. Her children were used to being 'only the three of them', and they were not happy with their mother's marriage. When Valerie learned that her son was hiding in the schoolroom cupboard rather than returning home, she decided to end the marriage, which was then less than a year old. Or perhaps the decision was made easier by the abortion he persuaded her to have, thus emphasising the fact that this was not the family life she had been seeking after all. It was not hard to face financial difficulty again because she had done it before and she believed she could succeed again, at least well enough to support herself and her children. She had not been married long enough for her contacts and skills and confidence to fade. Moreover, her children had not only grown accustomed to her working but had developed in accordance with the necessity of working. Her son had gone through periods of trying to manipulate her – he would routinely be sick before she left on a business trip, thus playing on her greatest fear, that of leaving her children when they needed her most, when only she could nurse them (as she had nursed her daughter through pneumonia after the doctor had given her up for dead). She joked with them, 'You're not allowed to be ill', because there was nothing like their illness to upset her routine. This is one of the primary problems about day care as opposed to au pair or nanny care, because an ill child cannot be left at a day-care centre – but it is possible that a nanny or child-minder would be sufficiently trustworthy to look after an ill child in his or her home. Her prohibition against illness was a joke, yet they understood its seriousness. When her tiny daughter fell off the porch and cut her forehead she got up immediately and shouted through the blood and tears, 'I'm sorry, Mommy. I'm all right, really.'

Children Support their Working Mothers

There is something poignant about children showing this kind of strength, yet children themselves value their ability to cope with the pressure put upon them. Valerie's daughter discovered her power to recover from injuries. She had the pride of someone able to participate in the adult world by helping her mother in this way. She saw that the best way to help her mother was to be independent. Child psychologist David Scharff claims that nothing frightens him as much as an independent child because that child has given up hope of attachment. He prefers to see a whining, clinging child, because that child at least indicates an awareness of possible comfort, even though he obviously feels that his source of affection is under threat. Dr Scharff clearly has good reason to say this, and he has observed many sad cases in which independence indicates emotional numbness or emotional poverty, but I have also found, among the children of the women I interviewed, a remarkable network of emotional support developed in spite of the haphazard and unsatisfactory conditions in which the children were cared for or 'minded'.

Child-minding – What is the Lesser Evil?

Motherhood is such a well-established institution that alternatives are rare and always less than stable. In the best of times it is difficult to find someone to look after the children – someone other than a mother, that is. The most determined and well-off women employ a full-time maid or nanny, and a part-time or back-up one, for holidays, or in case of illness. But money is no guarantee of finding a suitable employee, and many professional women have been struck by the cost, in terms of time and effort, of finding and keeping someone suitable. In America the English nanny is considered ideal – she would be one of the few English-speaking child-minders who could be relied upon, and so professional American families go to enormous lengths to secure visas for nannies – after first having gone to the trouble of flying over to England to interview and select a nanny. When the nanny arrives she will discover she is part of an elite. If she joins a group of other English nannies, she will learn of her special position and confront her employer with new demands involving which hours to work, which jobs are suitably hers. She probably wants to earn more money, and so she takes on other child-minding jobs, which may interfere with the needs of her first employer. One only needs to look at the advertisements in various magazines to see how high a turnover there is among posts for nannies and child-minders – and a high turnover indicates a high level of dissatisfaction on the part of one or both parties. More dependable is the foreign nanny – usually from the Philippines – who serves one well in the home and is loving towards the child, but who does nothing to stimulate the child's language skills. Or there are maids, usually black – my family employed one when I was a child, as did the families of many of my friends – who are adult fixtures in the house, but who are given no real responsibility for the child. In Britain there is a wider use of au pairs, who confront one with the embarrassment of being one of the family and employed by the family. The employer is *in loco parentis* but her authority is used towards making her own life easier. Some au pairs have little experience with children and are too young to be responsible. Some are excellent, but their time with a family is usually temporary. Moreover, they are supposed to work only five hours a day, so this would not suit a full-time working mother. Child care in day-care centres may be more reliable, but it always carries with it the danger of cross infection, and most mothers who use day-care centres put up with many colds, flus and often worse. The one private full-day child-care centre in Northwest Washington was struck by an amoeba that could be cured only by administering arsenic just below lethal dosage, and one mother who contracted the amoeba from her son had to choose between enduring the symptoms for six months and having an abortion – since she could not be treated while pregnant. Her son, who continued to attend the centre, contracted the amoeba three times, and three times had to endure the awful treatment.

Women who are forced to work from sudden financial necessity can rarely afford nannies or private day-care centres. Local authority service departments in Britain provide full-time day nursery places for 30 500 children, yet there are 172 000 children whose mothers are out to work for more than thirty hours a week. Moreover, these places are usually reserved for children labelled 'at risk', those who suffer neglect or cruelty. Most parents of very young children rely on child-minders, many of whom are unregistered, though registration carries no guarantee of their suitability, and many who are unregistered are just fine. Child-minders are much cheaper than nannies, but they often provide a minimum of care, and seldom look after children who are over seven years old. Therefore many children whose mothers work as breadwinners, or primary contributors to the family income, become 'latchkey children' — that is, children who come home from school and let themselves in with their own to key to an empty house. Inevitably this is a lonely experience, and it can be harmful, leading children to seek any company at all rather than face an empty house. It denies them the supervision they may need, especially as young teenagers. It is not a good system, and most mothers were unhappy with this arrangement, but believed they had no choice. Most children, too, disliked this arrangement, but they were able to develop strong emotional ties to one another, and to learn how to accept domestic responsibility, and responsibility for one another. One boy who looked after the house and his sister from four o'clock, when they returned from school, until seven or eight at night when his mother — a divorced woman now working as a civil servant — returned, spent his time constructing ways he might protect his sister and escape the house if it were burgled or burnt. In another family, a girl was always the first to come home, and she would hide in a corner until her older brother appeared. She then said that they always fought — which was probably a way of releasing the tension of having been alone. Sometimes the brother would hit the sister (she meant to exasperate him!), but she agreed not to 'tell' on him if she could then play with a friend she was not supposed to see. It was clear that the mother's plan for them to babysit each other was not working in the way she had hoped, yet it did seem to be working

116

for them. There were rules they would not allow one another to break, but these did not always coincide with the mother's rules, especially when those rules seemed arbitrary to them. Their independence encouraged them to develop a child's adult-like world, which they kept separate from their mother, but which helped her because it allowed them to survive in the conditions she needed for survival. As a latchkey child myself, I know that it is not the tragic system many make it out to be – nor is it dangerous. There has never been any correlation found between latchkey children and delinquency. The loneliness it can generate is not overwhelming, and, so far as I could see, it fostered not cold independence and unmanageability, but strong bonds between siblings and a sense of their role in domestic management.

Necessity as Luck

After Valerie Wade's divorce, she left New York for Denver. The schools there, she had heard, were the best in the country. She opened a shop which in time became known as the little Gumps (a well-known shop in San Francisco). Her career changed direction several times, but she was always sufficiently successful, and all her moves were characterised by that initiative and fearlessness women require if they are to have any chance at balancing their needs. And, having had her children at such a young age, Valerie had a large chunk of adulthood left when her children were grown. She was in her early thirties when her daughter was married and her son was in the army. We have all seen women who are empty after their children leave home. The new direction, the new emphasis their lives must now take, can generate anxiety and a sense that one has not made what one should from one's previous life. Even healthy, active women, with a good many interests, can be seen to employ means of making demands upon their families on the grounds of what they have given them in the past. This is a sure sign of dissatisfaction, of the knowledge that one has been cheated oneself. Valerie had certainly given a good deal to her children, and worked for them, but she had also worked for herself, and when they were grown she simply sat down, looked around her empty apartment and said, 'Right. Once I worked for them. Now what I do is for my-self.' This is the healthiest and happiest outcome of working as a result of necessity.

Valerie Wade's youth and naïvety were advantageous to her, but even when a woman is confronted with the need to support herself and her children later on in life, the necessity can stimulate courage – though this is difficult to do unless the woman has some preparation for a career. Julia Walsh, like any good army wife, quit her job in Washington when her husband was transferred to Kansas, but before she and her family left Washington, he was killed on manoeuvres. She was thirty-four, and had four sons, be-tween eight years and eleven months old. She did have some savings – twenty thousand dollars – but that seemed little to her in contrast to what she would need, so she took the money and invested it in four promising stocks. 'It was the only time I was really reckless', she claims, but her recklessness was not blind. She had worked with a securities firm, though then – in the late 1950s – women stockbro-kers were rare, to say the least. She had displayed clear talent for the market in business school, and one of her teachers had had the courage to employ her in his firm. Indeed, she had around her a strong support system. Though she had many disadvantages as an army wife and as a woman of her time (she was immediately expelled from the Foreign Service upon her marriage simply because a married woman could not hold a job), her husband encour-aged her to attend George Washington Business School when they moved to Washington, even though she was pregnant, and her mother-in-law, who lived with them, not only joined her son in encouraging her but actively helped by looking after the children. (The mother-in-law had battled with her own family to go away from home to uni-versity. And the legacy of her success was passed on to the son, who appreciated the expansive needs of women, and to the daughter-in-law, who benefited from the son's outlook and the mother-in-law's help.)

Within eighteen months, Walsh's stocks had quadrupled, and she bought her own home in Washington, where she still lives. But like all women who have the luck of knowing where their talents lie, and who have the good fortune, too, to honour their talents by making them effective, the lump sum of money, which might have tided her over, did not appear as a promise of security. Only work, only an on-going career could provide her and her family with what she and they needed. Independence is not so much a matter of money in the bank, but of earning power, and the skills and activities that go with that power. Julia Walsh realised immediately that she required a life of her own after her husband died, and a life of one's own, in our society, involves having a career. There may be exceptions, but this is the rule. There may be better societies, wherein women can have a full sense of themselves and their purpose without having a marketable career. Maybe, in time, this society will change a little. But as things are now, our self-respect depends upon joining the workforce in some way, and joining it to our advantage, being able to master the skills which run the workplace. It is in this sense that women must develop a more 'masculine' outlook.

When Julia Walsh was starting her career as a stockbroker, however, she was continuously reminded that she was a woman, and therefore a freak as a stockbroker. To reinforce her boss's decision to hire her she had to take some tests gauging her knowledge of the market. She showed a high score, but she says that she had to accommodate herself to prejudice against her. She simply was not taken seriously. She behaved less aggressively in her job than she would have liked, cultivating a sedate appearance and choosing safe investments, even though she knew from her own experience that she could succeed even when she took greater risks, and she would therefore have liked more adventurous clients. She never became part of the old boy network, but eventually she did become one of the very few women to sit on the board of the American Stock Exchange. Like the much younger lawyer Barbara Thomas, she appears as a conservative woman so that people will think they know what to expect of her. This is a line women still take, and most of them feel that it is not so much giving way to prejudice against women as playing according to the rules of a professional woman, just as men have learned to play their way, and dress in a certain style, according to the image they hope to project.

Women who work because they must support their families, work for their families in a more immediate way than does the man who advances his career 'for the wife and children'. Julia Walsh had the power to pay back help in the best way possible – that of passing on her talents to her children. She had not had much support from her parents. They were a traditional Irish–Catholic couple living in a small midwestern town, and though her mother gradually became resigned to her daughter's independence, her father, she reports, resented it. But the family she chose as an adult gave her tremendous support, and a person who feels that she has been lucky with the people around her, that she has done well because of them, tends to become generous, too. Whereas the crush of responsibilities upon Valerie Wade, which she had carried alone, led her to feel relief when her children were grown, and allowed her to consider herself first – a new luxury – Julia Walsh, who had family support even while she struggled as a single mother, and who was lucky enough to expand that family when she remarried (her second husband was a widower with six children), changed directions by forming her own company – but a family company, Julia Walsh and Sons. She continues to work with her children, as boss of course.

Independence is a false ideal. What can we be working for, if we work only for ourselves, and think only of ourselves? But it is also wrong to think that working, developing one's own skills and one's own career, is simply doing something for oneself, as opposed to working in the home, which is allegedly on others' behalf. In working ourselves we are becoming something that will have meaning to our children, and we are protecting them from our own helplessness, which we would otherwise probably have to face at some time in our lives. Child-rearing at its best is shared between at least two adults, but the mother who feels herself to be the primary parent may well want to know something about how her life would be, financially and emotionally, without her children's father. It is silly, I think, to follow Colette Dowling's recommendation to be totally independent always, to pretend we never have the support of the father, just because there is always the possibility that we will lose that support. We may have the luck to balance our needs more evenly, and more easily, when we have the help — to which we are entitled — of the father. But we also need to experience some mastery over that working world, which is both close to us and yet, because we may have limited skills, foreign to us. We should not put ourselves in a position in which independence fills us with terror.

8
Star Performers

The Satisfied Egoist

Isn't there a type of success that waylays all difficulties? Doesn't fame, in this society which so often sees fame as an end in itself, protect one from certain doubts? Celebrity can become a cloak which keeps out ordinary self-criticism. When narcissism finds such exultant satisfaction, it becomes reluctant to give way to others. I imagine the unstable marriages of those in the Hollywood clan to be the result of a rampant egoism, one which simply will not be modified by others' views – and domestic life demands curbs upon vanity, and acceptance of others' criticism, a willingness to bend to it, and to gauge the rightness of one's own needs in relation to others' needs. Yet movie stars, I suppose, are people too, and when they become mothers, their narcissism is undermined, at least in regard to one person. These women, too, change when they become mothers, and feel the duress of motherhood (the Swiss Ursula Andress reported that she broke into tears just at the mess caused by her infant son) and its special pleasure. Diana Rigg claimed that she no longer went out in the evening, but chose to stay at home and 'bite her daughter's bottom'. Lindsay Wagner found that much of the anger which had plagued her since adolescence was magically dissolved at the birth of her child. Far more down to earth, British actress Felicity Kendal said, 'Of course my child comes first, but that doesn't mean I'm going to read her stories every night, instead of working.' Esther Rantzen made an issue of nursing her first daughter in public, thus showing, in celebrity fashion, the pride of maternity.

It is usually said that the only purely selfless love is maternal love, because it is wholly directed towards another; and at the same time it is said that maternal love is purely selfish because the mother is looking upon the child as (part of) herself. Yet what women fear most when faced with the prospect of motherhood is losing themselves. In psychoanalytic terms, this may be explained by their sense of being overwhelmed by their own mothers – motherhood evokes memories of their own infancy, and of their infantile response to their mother – but in practical terms, in the terms in which it is experienced by women, it is a fear of being overwhelmed by the child. The woman knows that as a mother she will no longer have the same kind of control over her own desires and priorities. She will no longer belong to herself in the same way. She may be isolated from the people around her not only because she is at home with the infant, but because she herself has changed and is no longer accessible to those around her in the way she used to be. Stars may have access to their previous selves through their public image. It is the immediate feedback of an audience, or the tangibility of a glossy portfolio, that diminishes the threat of loss. The joys, the stresses, the sacrifices are tinged with unreality. They become shadows of the more private woman's troubles. They are expressed in an uncommon language, whose truth I cannot gauge.

But when I was more sympathetic to the efforts that lay

behind the celebrity, when I saw that celebrity as a by-product of challenge and excellence, I could see more easily the human story, and I was able to choose two very different personalities to look at the different ways the stresses and satisfactions of life as a star performer can modify and intrude upon one's life as a mother. Kiri Te Kanawa and Lynn Seymour have both had the opportunity to have every narcissistic need satisfied by an adoring audience, and they are both mothers. One smoothly balances her dual life. The other lives always on the brink of self-destruction, craving and risking more than life can bear.

The Talent that Changes Personality

Talent is an undeniable incentive, but in neither of these highly talented women was their talent discovered without a highly biased method of seeking for it. Kiri's mother chose a name which meant 'bell', and since she believed her natural father had a lovely tenor voice, she was confident that Kiri would sing, too. But Kiri's dedication was touch and go until she had her first public success at Covent Garden in 1969. She had been well known, and popular, in her native New Zealand before that, but, as she knew, she was loved partly because she was from New Zealand, and the continuing appreciation at home did not require the full stretch of her ability. Her first performance as the Countess in *The Marriage of Figaro* brought international recognition. The London critics proclaimed the birth of a star. Kiri was exultant, and in the initial headiness believed that she was destined to be admired, as she was in New Zealand, with a minimum of effort. She did not attend her scheduled singing lesson the next day. She was a star, after all, and needed no teaching. But during the second performance she became aware of the strain of competing with her previous performance. This second performance was broadcast, so her teacher heard this one too (she had been in the theatre the first night), and, when Kiri asked her what she thought of it, expecting to be greeted with more praise, Vera Rozsa replied that it had not been as good as the first, that perhaps she was tired or something. Having become overnight too good for anything but adulation, Kiri was furious and declared that she never wanted to see her teacher again. After the third performance, John Copley, the producer, also told Kiri that she was below par. She denied this hotly. It had been brilliant, she told him. But, Copley reports, the next performances were brilliant. In spite of her initial impulse to deny criticism, she took it to heart. She returned to her teacher. She learned how to work at a part, so that the 'luck' of a single splendid performance could be repeated. She learned that awful discipline of judging one's own performance, and accepted the stress of continuous work. Her success became a challenge, not a narcissistic blockade.

Kiri is not naturally disciplined. She is thoroughly extrovert, and can still be distracted by the pleasures of friends, cooking and entertaining; but her mother's determination that she develop her ability, and the good fortune of both mother and daughter that the mother had rightly guessed where the girl's talent lay, helped her along. She had too that extra push a father may give his daughter when he must turn his special attention to her as the son he never had. The model of the successful woman as either the oldest daughter or from a family of all daughters who becomes close to her father because he has no son upon whom to direct his ambition and his good paternal energies, was, twenty years ago, frighteningly, relentlessly valid; but though this is no longer so common that we can see it as a model, it can give a daughter that extra ability to take herself seriously, to see herself and her life in a wider context. But when one asks what the father did when he treated his daughter 'like a son' it usually means that he did not approach her with the assumption that she would be limited. He found a companion in her, and did with her the things he liked to do. In Kiri's case it was her mother who was ambitious for her, and her father who simply did with her what he would have done with a son, had he had one – he took her fishing and taught her to play golf and assumed that she would grow up to be independent.

Another important influence in Kiri's life was her

knowledge that she was adopted. When the social worker first brought the five-week-old baby girl to her parents, they rejected her on the grounds that they wanted a boy. But when the social worker returned a few weeks later, having found no other home for her, they felt sorry for her and took her. When she was two years old she was told that she was adopted. This would be an alienating experience for any child, however loved she felt by her adoptive parents. The child understands that her natural parents did not want her. Even though this is not always the case – a child may be put up for adoption because she has been orphaned – the child always feels that this is so. Kiri, however, turned this alienation into an asset. It made her feel that she was special, that she had been singled out for something. She is sure that she would have stayed in New Zealand 'breeding children' if she had not had this sense of being different, of needing to fight back and prove herself.

Every child has fantasies about parents who are grander, more important, nobler than the parents with whom the child is actually living. Freud called this the family romance – the child's fairy tale of royal descent. Freud believed that in fantasy the child harkened back to the time when the mother and father did appear as king and queen – or whatever is the equivalent in the infant's mind. Parents were once seen to be omnipotent and omniscient, but as the child grows she understands their weaknesses, their limited power within the society, and their relative insignificance. We are too good, we think, to have sprung from such common origins. Our true selves reside in a higher genealogy. An adopted child can dwell longer within this fantasy, which is what Kiri did, but like many myths about one's self it was not idle daydreaming but a dream to be realised in actual life. She never made any effort to meet her natural parents, but she clung to a sense of specialness. For until very recently a woman who planned her life in terms of a career, and who hoped for success in a profession, had to think of herself as different. It is not that Kiri's profession has a prejudice against women – a certain number of female opera singers are necessary to the profession – but often women singers, as students, were not taken seriously because people thought they would not develop into professional singers. (Gwyneth Jones, the Welsh soprano, was once refused a local grant for further study because it was thought that though she had talent she would return home after college and simply get married and have children. She has married, and she does have a child, and neither of these have retarded her career.) And in many ways Kiri appeared to be a 'typically' undedicated young woman who happened to have a lovely voice. She often did not turn up for classes at the London Opera Centre, offering one invalid excuse after another, such as 'The car broke down', when she had not been in a car, or she 'had a headache' or a 'sick friend', and John Copley once had to send her home from a rehearsal of *The Magic Flute* because she did not know the words. Even after her first Covent Garden success she had to refuse the offers that came pouring in because she simply did not know very many roles. But she has fought back, meeting the challenge of her talent, because she has always harboured the sense of being special. She has a confidence that will overcome any lack of dedication. When she was advised to cancel the first night of *Arabella* because, ten days before the opening she did not know the part, she refused. She locked herself in a room, put headphones on, stared at the score, and learnt the part perfectly. Her ambivalent dedication does not defeat her because she does not give up. She will never give up on herself, and therefore she will be all right.

Kiri married early on in her career, and she chose as a husband not her fiancé from home, with whom she admits to having been very much in love, but Desmond Park, an Australian engineer, who, she believed – and rightly – would stabilise her, increase her dedication and protect her from her own tendency to be distracted. They wanted to have children, and she did become pregnant, but she then miscarried. They soon decided to adopt a child, and did so, after which she became pregnant again. When she again miscarried, she admitted to being relieved because she had been worried about coping with one adopted and one natural child. They have since adopted a second child, a boy, and Kiri is delighted with both of them. Having been adopted herself it is not surprising that she finds having adopted children just as satisfying and natural as having her own children. In fact, even the bonding of motherhood, which is genetic in origin, which stems from the biosocial impulse to care for children who have one's genes, is not based upon the fact of those children having the parents' genes, but on the adult's response to any child in her care. Because the child in her care is usually a child who contains half her genes, she responds to any child in her care as though the child had her genes. The biosocial backing for the institution of motherhood works for adopted parents and their children, too.

Talent Forged by Determination

Lynn Seymour, the Canadian ballerina, reveals a temperament totally different from Kiri Te Kanawa's. She was always determined to succeed, and was always a hard worker. Lynn was so serious as a student that some people considered her stiff, stand-offish. She did not mix well with her peers, and she used this sense of isolation to give her the necessary sense of specialness, of being set apart, which many women need in order to believe they will not follow the usual pattern of being exclusively a mother, and allowing motherhood to engulf their expansive needs. Lynn Seymour obviously has talent, but she also has many natural handicaps. Her body is not, physically, well suited to dancing. She does not have the taut muscles and fine tone of someone like Antoinette Sibley, a fellow student in London. Her feet are not strong or well arched, and she has, since childhood, been plagued by one defeating injury after another. Yet she was determined to be a dancer, and she has recovered from every injury, through tremendous effort, and with the help of a teacher who specialises in nursing injured dancers back to work.

Lynn does not follow the once typical pattern of the successful woman any more than does Kiri. She is not the oldest child, and she is not from a family with no sons. Her older brother, who ran for Canada in the Commonwealth games, and who set a high standard as an academic as well as an athlete, did not absorb the family's ambition and goals, but instead acted as a stimulus. Her mother fostered her independence, in a myriad of small, sometimes indefinable ways, although they were very close, and although homesickness, or despair at separation from her mother, was the greatest drawback to her work in London. And Lynn, like so many successful women, claims that her father treated her as a son. Her explanation for this is that her father had a very poor relationship with his own mother, who burdened him with her neediness and her emptiness, and that he therefore rejected the notion of a daughter who would be domestic and home-oriented in the way his mother was. Instead, he offered her a sense of adventure he had inherited from his father, whom had had loved dearly. By relating stories of the courage and daring of her grandfather, he widened her vision of herself and her own potential.

The Shaping Decision

Many young women have a sense of themselves as being special, of having a value which has not yet been realised. All young people should have this belief in their good potential, whether or not they have objective reasons for their beliefs. It is this confidence alone which can overcome both the threats from within – our wish for self-punishment, our fears of being challenged, of testing our abilities, of setting ourselves up and therefore being in danger of someone knocking us down – and the inevitable disappointments from without which we must modify and refuse to see as a final dismissal of our efforts. But for this confidence to work, it has to be directed. We have to aim at something and, especially when we are very young, adults close to us can help us see a direction and help us understand the implications of our choices. The role of mentors in making a young person more pragmatic in her outlook – that is, showing her how one choice affects another, how one path will lead to this or that, or prove to others this or that – is invaluable, and both Kiri and Lynn had teachers who were patient with their particular limitations and worked with them to overcome them, thus enforcing that confidence which may at times have appeared to be irrational. As very young women, too, both of them had special help from their parents because the parents saw the cost of pursuing a profession and wanted to be sure that the girl knew what she was doing, that she understood the cost, understood that it was not necessary, but that if the cost was paid there should be no turning back. It was in neither case a simple matter of financial investment – though that was part of it – but of making sure that the girl was on top of her choice. Kiri was still working in her home town in New Zealand, and in the process of applying for a grant which would have stood part of the funds for her London study. Her parents put it to her that she had just one chance – either she sang, or she continued with her present modest job, but whatever she did, she had to see the decision as final, and give herself to whatever way of life she chose. She reports herself as saying, 'Okay, I'll take it – let's give it a go', but she also understood the seriousness of the claim and says that 'from then on I haven't stopped'.[1] For Lynn Seymour, this decision, as every other in her life, was more difficult, involving greater cost and greater unhappiness. She was in London, suffering from enormous homesickness, and just recovering from a foot operation. Her mother, who knew of her depression, said she would have to make a definite decision. Would she continue with her career as a dancer, or would she be returning to Canada? Could she cope with her homesickness? Could she overcome it? She wrote back that it 'broke her heart to make this decision' but she wanted to be a dancer and she knew she could not be one in Vancouver. She understood that if she did return home to be a 'normal' schoolgirl she would be weeping and wailing within a week. Being away from home was, after all, a sacrifice she was willing to make.

This type of commitment helps a young person through heartache, and prevents heartache from turning to vacillation, but it is not the whole story. There will be setbacks in confidence and reassessment of costs, and for someone who is a performer in the arts, these periods are particularly difficult. In a short story, Thomas Mann describes an acrobat whose performance is so professional, so perfect – and it must be so, since her life depends upon it – that it is impossible to imagine her having a life offstage. Not only must her concentration during performance be absolute, but all her energy must be reserved for the performance. She may be an ordinary wife and mother offstage, but the narrator in Mann's story claims he cannot imagine it, because the demands of the performance are so exhausting. An artistic performer does face this pressure. Whereas a lawyer or business executive can get away with an off day, or retire to a lower level of energy for a time, a performer, as long as she is a performer, is always at full stretch. Lynn says that being on stage is torture. She can never be sure that she will not fall over and sit down. If she gives a careful performance she will be doing nothing interesting. Without risk, a performance is lifeless – and one can see this in her projection of defiant vulnerability. Yet both she and Kiri most definitely do have a life offstage. Kiri's offstage life is so important that she describes her singing as her 'job' – not her life, which is made up of family and friends. And Lynn's offstage life is characterised by the same searching passion we see in her dancing.

These star performers are mothers, too, and I think if anyone has an easy time of things, in terms of a naturally easy-going temperament and an ability to take things as they come, and take them in good humour, Kiri does. She is not one to make herself suffer. She is not one to fret or to brood guiltily over her divergent needs. But like all women who become mothers, she did suffer a crisis of dependency versus expansive needs. Following her first miscarriage, Kiri contracted hepatitis and, following that, something diagnosed as anxiety depression. Hepatitis is an infectious, not a functional, disease – that is, it has a physical not psychological or emotional cause; but it does seem to be tied to emotional effects, just as our emotional state can make us more susceptible to an infection. Hepatitis tends to linger, and one of its symptoms is lassitude. Recovery is slow, and even when the infection has cleared there is a long-term loss of energy. This then is similar to depression, and it is often experienced as depression. Lack of energy may lead to anxiety and stress – because there are so many things we want to do, and think we should do, but we simply can't. Miriam Stoppard, the medical writer and television personality, suffered from hepatitis when she was working in a medical firm and dealing with her children, and the slow recovery, the loss of energy – even though she was in a position to view it with supremely informed objectivity – led her to reassess her goals. She decided that she had been drawing too heavily upon the 'love bank' of her husband and sons and that it was time to pay something back. She resigned from her job, and changed the direction of her career (this was when she started the television series, *Where There's Life* . . .), because the pressure of her previous life had seemed at a dead end. She had been giving too much to her 'job' but she could not, as a result, simply turn completely to her family, pretending that she had no other needs. She did, however, have to refresh herself with a change, and find a different kind of career pressure.

Kiri's depression was linked to her miscarriage, but it was also linked to her growing distance from her husband. It had been difficult for him to see Kiri's increasing success – not that he resented it, but like most men, he had the commonsense to see that he needed job satisfaction too. So while she had been singing in New York and Paris, he was working in Western Australia. Her illness forced her to stop work, and she spent her convalescence with him. They had grown apart, but they were still a couple, and still loved one another. Whereas he found it difficult to stay beside her when she seemed to be deriving her life from her job, when he saw her need he gave up his job in Australia and went into business for himself so that he could adjust his schedule to fit hers – and this now allows him to spend time with the children when she has to be away. Kiri says she hates being away from the children for any length of time, but her 'hatred' seems to be a healthy missing of them, not anxiety, not guilt. She learned how to balance her needs just before she became a mother, and her easy-going nature keeps this in check. Some great singers, who are also mothers, keep to a severe regimen because of their children. Yvonne Minton limits herself to twenty-five performances a year so that she can spend time with her children, and Valerie Masterson took off two full years to bear and nurture her children. Janet Baker refused to become a mother because she guessed that she would have developed a strong maternal tie, and would therefore not have been able to give her voice what she knew it deserved.

We Can Have It All

It is possible to do these things – to have a career, even one as a star performer and to be a mother – without torturing oneself. For a time even Lynn Seymour was calm about it. After her twins were born she told an interviewer who asked about her career and her children, 'You make it sound like the Second World War. I only get frazzled occasionally. They're marvellous to come home to. I feel sorry for mothers who have to stick at home with the kids all day. I think it's nice for the children that I'm not there all the time. I'd become a bore. This way we see each other fresh.'

Here indeed we have all the good news about being a professional and a mother. Yes, there are hectic times, but these are not the rule. Any mother has hectic times, anyway, and the woman who stays at home with the kids may suffer more because she has no reprieve, no chance to walk out of the house and breathe fresh air. Instead, the working mother sees her children not as a job but as a pleasure. They are after-work entertainment. They provide comfort from the stress of work. They remind one, after the demands, the quarrels, the competitions, that one has an implacable human centre, that one matters even if one should fail 'out there' because one's importance to one's children – and vice versa – is impervious to the outrages of career fortune. Finally, we have the argument that the children are better off with the mother at work. When she is always at home she loses interest for them. She becomes no more than a source to satisfy – or to refuse to satisfy – various requests.

Both children and mother dwell upon irritations while they develop excessive dependencies upon one another – false dependencies resulting from claustrophobic habits.

Yes, there may be long stretches of time in which the positive side of both working and mothering may be the only side seen; but there are times, too, when we have to work hard to see the good at all. And even when things are going very well, even when the balance comes easily, we should know that it won't always be easy. Our children sometimes need to take us for granted more than they need to find us interesting. They need our attention, and often the self-absorbing teenage years, just when we think they are grown and our intense maternal duties are at an end, are the worst. Sometimes the few hours we have with them after work are glorious, leading us to speak of 'quality time', but 'quality time' still involves time, and when we dedicate ourselves to a career, too, we may find ourselves with no time. When we return from work we may be fresh neither to them nor to ourselves – we may simply be tired. And the times that are good may be the too-good-to-be-true times of a honeymoon, which remain an unfinished story. It is this kind of happiness which many working mothers have with their children, until everything is turned upside down and they become anxious over not having enough, and seek a change in their schedule.

If there are difficulties to be met in a situation, there is no doubt that Lynn Seymour will meet them. As Ninette de Valois, one of her first teachers, said, she has 'a streak of independence and largesse of personality that – as in all such cases – does more for others than for the individual concerned'. Lynn does not make life easy for herself. We can stand back and admire Kiri's general life ease, but we can learn more from Lynn, who meets every bump head-on. Her sense that she was doing it all was a temporary 'high'. She knew her children would enforce rests from her career, and she knew she needed them, simply because the type of intensity her dancing demanded from her could not be continually met, especially as her particular talent is bound up with the other needs in her life. This strongly individual character of her dancing has brought her luck, furthering her career, because it was so much what choreographer Kenneth Macmillan needed as an inspiration – and Lynn's first great success came when she danced in Macmillan's *The Invitation*, portraying a girl destroyed by the violation of her awakening sexuality. But it also frightens her, and she does not always want to meet its demands. She claims, for example, that she got pregnant the first time in order to have an excuse not to dance. Subsequently, pregnancy and children came to be seen as a primary need. She now says that her children give her 'everything – plus perspective'. It is a remarkable claim for a professional woman to make, and if taken out of the context of her life it would appear as an exaggeration. They obviously do not give her everything – why does she obviously need so much more – from her work, from her men, from her self? But most mothers would know precisely what she means. They give her 'everything' in the sense that they could not give her more of what they do give her. When she is with them, when she holds them, they anchor her in their lives, so that nothing is more important than they are – which is not to say that nothing else is important to her. There is a sense of supreme importance which does not mean that one cannot bother about anything else. It is a matter of seeing what gives our whole life meaning, not a matter of devoting ourselves only to this, and being satisfied only by this. Children give her everything – plus perspective. The perspective may be in seeing how important small things are. The world may be falling apart, society destroyed, but a child is intent upon, and cheered by, the special way a ribbon feels, or he may perceive a popped balloon as a tragedy. Children offer the perspective of the immediate and insignificant, as well as a profoundly human perspective, whereby achievement and recognition are temporarily relieved of their command. The fact that her children give her perspective is a sign that her perspective is always changing, and the 'everything' that they give her is found in moments, and in general priorities – leading her, for example, to resign as choreographer in the Munich ballet when the children found it difficult being

separated from one another (she took her youngest son to
Munich with her while the older twins remained at school
in England) as well as being separated from her. This was
not the only reason for her resignation – it was a difficult
job, and her colleagues seemed set against her from the
start, making it very difficult for her to put any ideas into
effect – but it made her resignation, in her eyes, far more
reasonable, and less like simply giving up. Her children,
while they are still young and in her care, prescribe limits
to her activities, but they do not define the purpose of her
activities. Because children are so important to mothers,
women can easily be confused by the implications of that
importance. Their importance can override almost anything
else, but we have got to get a clearer idea of when they do,
rightly, override other things, and when we are simply giving in to the practical difficulties which arise because
motherhood is such a deeply ingrained institution and it is
therefore troublesome to find other means of taking equally
good care of the children. We also have to learn to see the
limits to the 'everything' that they give us, because if we
sentimentalise their needs for us and our duties to them, we
will cripple ourselves, as so many women have been
crippled. The tragedy of motherhood is that it is not a sacrifice for nothing, but an unnecessary sacrifice for something
of overwhelming value. It is so difficult, to weigh up needs
and balance our lives because motherhood cannot be dismissed as useless, yet we have few guidelines as to its real
uses, or to our real and absolute uses as mothers. It helps
to have an independent, perhaps only half-conscious drive
for achievement – as so many of these successful working
mothers do – so that one makes the right decisions even
when one thinks one is not. Repeatedly, after the injuries
that plagued her, Lynn Seymour doubted that she would
make a comeback. Even if the physical damage was re-
paired, she doubted that she would have the energy to return to the stage. But she did, until, facing her third
marriage and the knowledge that she could now have no
more children (she had had a hysterectomy), the risk her
dancing put to her personal life was too great, and she an-

136

nounced that her ballet career was at an end. Well, we have dependency needs, too; and we are lucky to have a chance to give into them. But Lynn did not give up work. Rather, she now works in tandem with her third husband, who is a rock and jazz promoter. Work is never easy to give up.

9
Dressed for Success

The Managerial Woman

That rare person – the female executive – was studied by
two women from the Harvard Business School, Margaret
Hennig and Anne Jardim, who found a remarkably consistent pattern in her life history.[1] She was the oldest daughter,
usually in a family with only daughters and not more than
three children. She was closer to her father than to her
mother, who tended to play a traditional role in the family.
The mother's limited vision and limited skills were a barrier
to intimacy with her daughter, who preferred the non-
domestic interests of the father, and who then formed a
bond with the father against the mother. These women
were threatened by any traditional female bonds and duties,

138

and were careful to avoid them. They did not marry until their mid-thirties, if they married at all, and then they married divorced or widowed men with children of their own, so that the closest they came to motherhood was as stepmother – a relationship which is seldom as complex and demanding as that of mother, however much genuine love and attachment grows from it.

These women not only protected themselves against commitments which might minimise their ambitions, but also trained themselves to think as men. They realised they fell down in seeing the overall picture of career progress, and would often fuss over a simple task, rather than slight one job in order to further a long-term goal. They had to overcome the compulsion to be 'nice' and the fear which made them inclined to step back from a battle. They learned to assert themselves without feeling ridiculous for being determined and self-assured. They assiduously avoided the self-sabotage of ambivalence about having a career, yet it is difficult not to see them as having sacrificed something else – those needs and capacities for nurturing children, and the ability to enjoy freely dependent relationships with men. For a woman who denies her dependency needs may be as lost and as limited as one who denies her expansive needs. Our lives deserve our best shot, not simply a series of intelligent defences.

The women Hennig and Jardim studied were all born in the United States, between 1910 and 1915. This was the generation of which Betty Friedan spoke in *The Feminine Mystique,* a generation which had no model for a woman who was both a professional and a wife and mother. This was the generation that saw only one woman doctor in their home town, and that woman was unmarried, wore sturdy shoes, had her hair cut short like a man's, and was overweight. These are the women psychoanalyst Dr Alexandra Symonds describes as harbouring 'neurotic dependencies', women who identify feminine traits with their 'despised self'. They reject the mother-training they got from their mothers. They reject their mothers and deny their dependency needs. In her practice Dr Symonds found many cases of neurotic anxiety – due to unresolved dependency needs – among successful professional women.

The New Managerial Woman

But what about the successors to Hennig and Jardim's women? Is not the woman business executive the model for the new spate of advertisements in the United States, showing the 'twenty-four hour woman', who brings home the bacon, cuddles her husband, reads bedtime stories to the children and wears an enticing perfume? Are there not so many such women that Betty Friedan was forced to decry their priorities in *The Second Stage*? Have women to-day not fallen prey to the feminist mystique, whereby they put careers first, and treat their families as at best an aside? In practice I found none. But in the corporate world, women came closest to this new stereotype. I found no very young women – most of them were born in the 1930s – because it takes time to become an executive. One firm in which I was conducting interviews had done its own research into the life history of the senior female executive.[2] According to this study of 600 women, the 'composite women senior executive' is still the first-born child in her family, but now often has one younger sister and one younger brother. She is not, as was her previous counterpart, from an all-girl family. Her average work week is fifty-three hours, which she considers to be comparable to her male peers – but given this work load it is not surprising to find that there are sharp differences in family status between her and her male peers. More than half of these women executives were unmarried, either because they had never married (28 per cent) or because they were widowed (4 per cent) or because they were divorced or separated (21 per cent). Nearly all the men however (95 per cent!) were currently married. This is still an area that clearly involves a kind of commitment which is at odds with a woman's family life, and these women knew it. They were not unmarried by accident. Those who were divorced or separated spoke of their career as an important factor in the breakdown of their marriage.

Most of these women did not have children. They achieved success in the old way, by foregoing family life. But 39 per cent of these women did have children, and of those who did have children most of them took primary responsibility for the child's care. When the husband did share a good part of the child care, it was an equal share, not a case of role reversal with the father taking on the mother's burden. I expected therefore to find women who were harassed, or who were partly inhuman in their supreme organisation – in the way Margaret Thatcher is. But instead I found an invigorating warmth and generosity combined with the ambition – to which they freely admitted. 'Of course I'm ambitious', Sandra Gillingham* laughed. At fifty-three she is a vice president of a New York bank. She has three children, and was divorced when she was in her mid-thirties. She describes her two sons and one daughter as 'beautiful. I love having them around. But of course they're grown now.' She had her first important job when her first son was 'a babe in arms. It caused no amount of domestic strife, believe me.' Her husband was living in Princeton, and she commuted to New York City. Her career began taking off when her husband was having difficulty with his. He was a rising executive in a retail firm which was liquidated, and he then spent some time searching for another job. During that time he did not help her with child care – and at the time she simply accepted this. It was difficult even to persuade him to allow her to pay for a maid who would care for the children while she was at work, but 'he was too down in the mouth to put up much of a fight'. She barely noticed her marital unhappiness because she was so happy with the children. 'And with my career, of course. I liked being busy.' She laughed again.

But there were some ropey times. Three children, remember, and no real nanny, just a daily maid who marked time with them. But because I was working and my work was going well, I felt in control. Maybe it was just in contrast to my husband, who seemed more and more weak to me, but I felt I knew where my life was going.

And a lot of my women friends got divorced at about the same time I did. But they were lost. When things got really bad it was easier for me to throw in the towel. The lucky thing was that he decided to leave me. Because he was so weak, I would have been afraid to leave him.

With these women, who were now in their fifties and whose children had grown, I had a strong sense of their having 'come through'. It was like being in a large room, full of fresh air. Certainly, they said their lives had been more difficult because they were women, but they did not feel that they were held back in their careers just because they were women. They faced a lot of petty 'male chauvinism' at work but mostly, they decided, because the men were simply unused to having women around and did not know how to treat them. 'Women are so political about every little thing', Sandra remarked. 'But I'm not sure it's really so much easier for a man. If a boss wants to sleep with a woman in payment for a promotion or salary rise then that boss isn't going to be fair to a man either. He's a rotter and he should be exposed.'

These middle-aged women executives, who seemed so brave and relaxed, none the less believed that one of the greatest obstacles to their success had been lack of confidence – this, they felt, was even more difficult than convincing others of their ability. But this was all water under the bridge. They had gained self-confidence along with experience and management training. They admitted to being a bit tougher because they were women, yet they also believed they were more soft-hearted than men (Sandra Gillingham would still have been with her weak husband if he had not left her) but that though they sometimes acted upon it (by working hard to find another position for someone whose work was not suitable to them) they were always careful not to show it spontaneously. They were self-conscious, too, or at least careful about their appearance. The British women tended to wear moderately smart clothes that were something like uniforms. The American executives favoured designer clothes, but it was often comic to see such expensive clothes put on with obvious haste or distraction, or in any case lacking the attention necessary to a 'smart' appearance. Jeanne Kirkpatrick, the US Ambassador to the United Nations, was quite put out when she was described by a Washington journalist as 'dumpy'. She protested that she went to fashion shows, and bought from the top designers; but in fact she often did look dishevelled – not unattractively so, but simply like someone whose mind cannot be on her appearance. Many of these women liked the texture and look of fine clothes, but they underestimated the amount of time necessary to come up to scratch as the model in an advertisement. Alas, they were too busy to exemplify the feminist mystique, which, as far as I could tell, was an advertiser's image, not one which functioned in anyone's life.

Does the Managerial Woman Raise Managerial Children?

Since the children of these women were young adults themselves I tried to talk about their lives as children of working mothers. Strangely, all the things the mothers worried about – the constant rush in the morning, the haphazard arrangements, especially during school holidays, the groans when they became ill (and children become ill so quickly – it is often necessary to change one's entire plans ten minutes before the journey to work is supposed to begin), the afternoons alone – seemed to be of no interest to the children. What many of them remarked upon, however, was how hard it had been for their mothers, and they were determined to avoid this. Most of the daughters I spoke to were determined to avoid this by not working when they had young children.

If this is a general response to the working mother, then the future looks pretty grim. Psychologists have told us that much of the confusions about motherhood stem from the fact that children are cared for primarily, and often exclusively, by women; and just when we hope to face a generation which will have avoided prejudices at an early age, we

143

find that generation turning itself into a previous model of mother and so putting back the process by two generations. And have not children learned, through their mother's lives, that independence is often necessary? One young law student, who claimed she was studying law because she liked to study and wanted to be a student for a while longer, rather than because she was planning a career, said that her mother, who had been divorced when she was three, had had to work so hard – 'I want to marry someone who will look after me.' But her mother had married – had that helped her mother? Marriage is not financial security. Her mother had learned that. Her mother had gained her own independence, but the cost seemed to the daughter too high.

The children of working mothers felt the burden their mothers carried and wanted to avoid it. What was so discouraging was that they had not thought through ways to avoid these burdens with any imagination. They wanted not to work when their own children were young. But how would this affect their careers? What careers were they planning? Like the law student who disclaimed specific ambition, most of them were doing things that looked as though they might result in a career. But since they already knew the cost, and since many of them wanted children, they could not quite admit to themselves that they were going to follow a similar path. The outlook is glum because the problem is so difficult, and these young women, who knew the difficulties, were forming defences against their future. Time alone will tell how these defences break down as they are either forced to work through financial necessity or feel the need to work themselves. It is unfair for us to expect so much of them, when we are only barely able to manage our own lives. We cannot learn lessons for them, and we should learn from them that we are not setting particularly good examples.

The children recalled more clearly than the women themselves the struggles they had endured – and the mothers, I suppose, were able to look back upon those difficult years with a sense of achievement – they had got through them, and survived, and they therefore had a new breadth, a new-found freedom in middle age.

These women thrived on having succeeded in a nearly impossible task. They were self-confident now because they had endured the years which demand a superwoman syndrome. Many women do not rise to the senior executive level in businesses because they are unwilling to take on the superwoman's task – a task which really means cutting down on domestic life. In the professions, too, this is so. One woman lawyer, working for the government, claimed that if she went into private practice, and was really to make a go of it, she would have to work between sixty and eighty hours a week, whereas with her two small children she simply refused to extend her fifty-hour work week. In the medical profession – both in organised medicine and in academic medicine – women do not achieve authoritative positions in proportion to their numbers simply because most of them trade career advancement for time to raise a family.[3] Most women physicians do have children (more than two-thirds) and plan to have children (85 per cent of female medical students plan to have children) but most of them are also primarily responsible for household tasks and child care.[4] One would expect more improvement in terms of help from fathers, but the help tends to be minimal and usually at the wife's specific request. It all makes Nora Ephron's remark highly plausible – that the one positive thing to emerge from the women's movement is the Dutch treat. But if this is extended to saying that women have learnt to pay their own way, then the lesson is not so small. To pay one's way, one must earn one's way, and to earn one's way one must develop marketable skills and one must learn how to market them. These are lessons we are still learning, but which we now have a better chance of learning and passing on to our children. But we must also learn, somehow, how to balance our lives. We must learn how to do this not simply in the sense of surviving difficult years and getting through it ourselves, but in the sense of learning how not to do it as superwomen, because it seems, the next generation is not interested in the superwoman scenario. Very sensibly, they see it as the ridiculous stunt it is, and they want something else.

A Child's View of Superwoman

I am the daughter of a superwoman, one of the early kind, the embattled woman of Betty Friedan's generation who had no back-up, no support from her women friends, and no desire to be friends with women because their interests and aims were so different from hers. She despised, under the guise of pity, women who thought only about keeping their house immaculate. And as for raising children – well, she did stay at home for four years when my sister and I were born. 'Talk about being bored', she remarked, commenting on those years, and it brought to mind the taste of boredom I had when she had been at home. Always she had been doing something else – painting the ceiling, or knitting interminably, or constructing shopping lists. She was always busy, and always bored. Yet children were an important part of her life, and as much as she despised women who did nothing but stay at home with the children, she despised equally a woman colleague who had not married or had children.

My mother was a doctor – an eye specialist – and a professor of physics. She was not only a freak of her generation – a mother who worked – but she was a freak within her profession – a woman doctor and scientist. She was always acutely self-conscious of her position, which in her eyes was elitist. Or rather, she saw herself both as a member of an elite and as a 'second-class citizen' – one of her favourite expressions. She knew she would be noticed, and she was highly anxious, in being noticed, to be found attractive. Unlike today's heroine who thinks it a sign of adverse discrimination if a man singles her out in a meeting to offer her a comfortable chair, my mother capitalised on such things. She wore bright colours, usually Pucci silks – those splendid, garish prints of the 1960s – flaunting her appearance, taunting men with it. That plain, overweight, unmarried female colleague did not draw fire as she did. She knew that her attractiveness, and her self-presentation, worked against her. She stimulated men only to complain that they thought about sex too much. She complained that they could never forget she was a woman, and yet she did everything in her power to remind them she was a woman. She knew if she played down her sexuality she might be more readily accepted, yet simultaneously she thought her sexuality was a trump, as though it would bring her the admiration she craved. So even as it worked against her, she valued it, and sought to preserve it, and tried to outshine all young female incumbents.

'A woman can do everything a man can do, and have children as well', my mother used to say, apparently reciting some creed. But to do everything a man can do did not mean that she would be a parent in the way that most men were. She was out to prove that she could do everything a woman could do, too. She made most of my clothes herself, passing on to me her corrupt appreciation for fine materials, for carefully mixed textures and patterns – all of which is far more personal than aesthetic appreciation, for it is linked to (and this is why I call it 'corrupt') a belief that one needs such things in order to be presentable, or that one can change oneself, make oneself better by the use of such decorations. My clothes were so special that people were bound to take note of them. 'Your mother made that?', my friends' mothers would ask in amazement. 'She made that, and she's an eye surgeon, a physicist . . . ' I saw them using the superwoman image to protect themselves from the competition. They were really generous towards her, far more than she was towards them. And it cost them nothing to appreciate her because if she was a superwoman, if she could do everything, then she was not a real, ordinary person, not a person whose life reflected in any way upon theirs.

The real unhappiness that lies behind the superwoman syndrome is not due to simple exhaustion or the stress of trying to do too much and to be too many things. It is not even due to living under the pressure of standards that are too high, or that are false – as when we think a good mother should make all her children's clothes and cook all the meals and be home every lunchtime. The real unhappiness is that the superwoman never believes in herself, never believes that she is truly successful, either in work or at home. The superwoman's aim is to prove her worth, but nothing is ever proof enough. The superwoman needs to be a star because she needs to be told she is marvellous. Therefore each small sign of recognition becomes terribly important. And no sign of recognition is enough, because there is no inward conviction.

The superwoman scenario is really an indication of female weakness because it caters to the prejudice that women have to be better than men in order to succeed as men succeed. Yet it is not surprising that the image of the superwoman arose along with feminism. The positive teaching of feminism is that women need to develop themselves in all areas, and to be treated by their teachers and parents and peers as though they shared with men a common professional potential. But if they become like men, then they will lose out – as men do – on their children. For all the battles that go on between mothers and fathers about sharing child care, there are very few women who actually envy the father's position with the children. Yes, half in jest, many women feel that it is unfair that they spend so much time with their children and the children end up adoring the father and taking the mother for granted. This is half in jest, because the real pleasure from being with children and caring for them is not simply in the love they happen, or happen not, to return. The satisfaction of maternal attachment is not in terms of return on input (if I do all this for them, then they will love me this much) but in the input itself. Mothers tend to have their children in a way fathers do not. They share in their lives, help make their lives, for better and for worse. And women do not want to give up this privilege. I remember my mother coming home from work, carrying two large bags of shopping, and before she could put them down we would come running to her, telling her this and that, asking her permission for this or that, desperate to get her attention, and make sure that she was tuned into us. My father's homecoming was an altogether different thing. We knew certain things were required for him. His needs came first, in typical patriarchal fashion. There was security, but there was also control, and we knew that we were in the background. But this gave my mother greater control over us, and this, obviously was what she wanted. As in the case of all people, one way of discovering what they actually want is looking at what they have got. Women want to be the prime parent, because it is rewarding and because it fulfils certain needs in them. As a result, when they fight for equal shares, their battle is often undermined by their own ambivalence. They affect the role of martyr, doing what they want to do but also demanding that other people feel sorry for them because they are doing so much. 'A woman can do everything a man can do and have children as well', but women have to accept that men can have children too. The cost of keeping them all to ourselves is, after all, too high.

The Feminist's Embarrassment

Many women, when they discovered the feminist movement, felt they had been feminists all their lives: my mother was one such woman. The feminist movement at first seemed to make sense of her battles. It confirmed her belief that in all sorts of ways, even with their flattery and deference, men were undermining her position, ensuring that she had no access to the true sources of power – all because they were afraid of women, afraid for their masculinity, afraid to be exposed as the weak and vulnerable people they were. She became, like many of the first 'libbers', politically sensitive to phrases, to assumptions underlining certain questions, yet she would still fall prey to being asked by a committee at the University of Northwestern as they considered her for an appointment, 'If you get this job what will your husband do for his breakfast?' Like any novice facing prosecution, she was both paranoid and ill-prepared. She wanted to be accepted as a professional, yet she appeared, in spite of her unquestionable qualifications, always to be acting the part. Like many women who knew they were different from most women, but who were unaware that they were the pioneers of a new movement, she was burdened with a self-consciousness that embarrassed other people even more than herself. I know that it embarrassed me.

When I asked Sandra Gillingham whether she thought her children suffered as a result of her career, she said:

> I think the only thing that really bothered them was the publicity. When I was made vice president it was at a time when this was really news, and I was on every chat show you can think of for a week. They hated me when I came home in the evening. 'Why did you say that?' my daughter asked. 'It made me cringe!' Everything I did offended them. They weren't in the least bit proud.

I knew what she meant. A famous mother is hard to take, usually because her fame is publicised far more personally than a father's fame. And this tends to embarrass the children. When Barbara Walters's daughter said that she felt protective towards her mother because her mother was hopeless at anything other than television, it struck me that this was an excellent defence against the mother's fame, an excellent way of coping with it, minimising it. But for the most part a mother's fame takes a child by surprise, and the fame is often presented as militant. The woman is a freak, and the child is embarrassed on her behalf. However genuine the mother's achievements, the urge a child has to take her mother for granted, and to see her in a domestic setting, makes her reject the mother's public acclaim.

The aggressiveness of the first feminists was necessary. A first voice must be a loud one. But just as daughters tend to be embarrassed by the publicity their mothers receive in a way they are not embarrassed by their father's publicity, the younger women who are sympathetic to the fundamental aims of feminism shy away from being 'feminists' because of the notoriety associated with that term. Recently, a journalist writing for the *New York Times* Magazine[5] discovered that in America, at least, where the movement was stronger and the current backlash more distinct – 'feminist' was a word to be shunned.[6] The first feminists, it seemed, had made the difficulties of female integration in the workplace more difficult because they made men acutely self-conscious. Every courtesy, every restriction was given a political interpretation. Women, it was assumed, were set up in opposition to men, and men had to be on the defensive. I know my mother certainly had this effect on men, and that because she was so vehement in her views I was very slow to honour the positive side of the feminist movement. The emergence of post-feminism, which reasserts differences between men and women and in many respects confirms beliefs about women that ten years ago were interpreted as propaganda of the oppressor, has a quieter and more tentative voice, but it is feminism's only hope of salvation.

The British v. American Personality

There is, I believe, an important difference between the majority of women who are now in their fifties and who gained professional success in the United States, and their peers in Britain. The former viewed their career and their success from a strongly egotistical viewpoint. They did not want to be deprived of independence – either financial or personal – nor did they want to be deprived of families. So they would have it all, and they laughed spitefully at the women who sacrificed one or the other. They were spiteful because they assumed that these women disapproved of them. These women had to flaunt themselves because they lacked support. Their new-found confidence, in middle age, when they no longer suffer the opprobrium of being inadequate mothers, is exhilarating, and it is usually accompanied by the realisation that their former appearance of confidence was a sham. But their peers in Britain seem to have a different psychological history. In Britain, the women I met were so serious about their work that they left the burden of self-consciousness far behind. Also, there was the tradition of the nanny to give them a head start when it came to being a working mother; and psychoanalytic theories, which led mothers to believe that the small tasks of child-rearing had an insurmountable effect on their children's lives and should be left to them alone, were never taken quite so seriously as they were in America. Also, there is in Britain a tradition of idealism of quite a different kind from the idealism of Americans, which tends to be short-lived, virulent and egotistic. The women in Britain who had attained marked success by the time they were middle aged were remarkably unself-conscious about their position as women, because their work came first, and the aims of their work dominated their thoughts, not their aims for themselves.

Elizabeth Anscombe was well known among British philosophers and considered so eminent in herself that people continued calling her 'Miss Anscombe' even after she became professor of philosophy at Cambridge, not to slight her academic position but to preserve a name that had in itself become a mark of distinction. She is a Catholic, and has seven children, and is very different from the Catholic women portrayed by contemporary novelists, from David Lodge to Marilyn French, who see the Catholic woman's life as crippled by repeated pregnancies. Professor Anscombe is a strong upholder of the Pope's encyclical on birth control, and is therefore quite unmodern in her no-nonsense association of sexual intercourse with the production of children. The cares which arise from having too many children – all those visits to the dentist or doctor, all those shoes to tie in the morning and clothes to wash in the evening – involve 'wisdom of the Flesh – and that is death'. This is hardly a view which suits contemporary thought, and many of her worldly-wise colleagues have laughed at her, but since even the popular mandate, Germaine Greer, is speaking out for a different kind of sex, a sex that is less 'free' and easy, Anscombe may get her hearing yet. Not that it matters much, because her beliefs are firmly entrenched in her life, and she lives happily by them.

Because she sees children as a 'given', not as something one always chooses to have, or not, she does not burden herself with fantasies about a mother's control over her children, and a responsibility for their well-being in a neat and middle-class notion of 'well-being'. She first became pregnant when she was a research fellow, living in College (her husband was teaching in another city at the time) and it was her tutor who, noticing the pregnancy, brought up the issue of the practical problems that might ensue. The rumour in Cambridge is that she told the tutor she planned to hang the baby from the window of her college room in a basket. Like many such anecdotal stories, there is a shred of truth – she knew that children needed fresh air, and she thought the tutor's concern was for the infant in a confined collegiate environment. She did not know precisely what a child would need, but she was confident that she would find this out when the child, and children, arrived. What is so impressive about her approach is that when she considers, 'How am I going to do it?', her query is made in the confidence that there is an answer. She sets out to solve the question, avoiding commonplace assumptions which would defeat her solution. The strength of her position comes from her knowledge that there was no way she could possibly have given up her philosophical work. Her strength comes from the fact that she does not feel herself, her work, to be threatened. The children that are born to her are not 'unwanted'. They are given to her. They are a natural outcome of the sexual aspect of married life. They are gifts for whom she must care, but her care is for the children as people, and, as people, it is unimportant whether they are organised in a conventional fashion, a fashion designed as much for the convenience of the mother as for the well-being of the children. Once Professor Anscombe got the 'bug' for philosophy, she knew she would not give it up. All souls are equal before God. She is as important as her children, and because there is a kind of fairness, or some guiding justice, in the spiritual world, those who do not mislead themselves into false values will be able to honour true values. Anscombe did not consider trade-offs as necessary. She solved problems as they arose, and worked alongside her children, encouraged her children to care for one another, and found the energy within herself to give her children the attention they needed, and still need, because she remains attached to them, and continues to see them in her care even as they have become adults. She displays a high-mindedness and purity and innocence that few of us could emulate, and her household is not one that many of us would want to imitate, but she can serve to remind us to reconsider what we assume is so important – a falsely controlled household, with a mother trying to enter the child's world in a Sesame Street fashion, entertaining the child by encouraging the child to see colourful toys and strange movements as an important part of her world, thinking one has accomplished something of note when the child can count to ten and recite the alphabet, overstimulating the child and strangely undernourishing her by not giving ourselves what we need. I know from experience that a child can see the mother's emptiness as she spends time with her child and neglects her own true interests. The boredom of the mother infects the child, and makes the child ask for more and more of the mother's attention, because the child does not understand what is lacking.

Upper-class Independence and the New Style

Shirley Williams, former Labour minister and co-founder of the Social Democratic Party, is thoroughly grounded in a tradition of independent women, though the number who thrive in this tradition is small. Her mother, Vera Brittain, was determined to break out of the roles assigned to women, and her determination and her sense of purpose paved the way for many women, among whom naturally was her daughter. Shirley Williams was used to being left with nannies, and in her autobiography her mother speaks of her anguish at leaving the baby Shirley, but she did leave her for weeks at a time, and Shirley Williams grew up with the assumption that families would work even though they were not always seen to come first. But times have changed, and it was often her husband who was left with their daughter while she went to political meetings, and in the end her family life did not thrive because, it seems, she took too much for granted. For all talk of the decline of the family, the demands for intimacy have actually increased in the last fifty years, and people feel justified in complaining that there is no domestic centre, no proper family life within a family. At one time, in Britain, the family structure could be more rigid, and its members more distant from one another, and it would still work – but this is far less common today. The break-up of Shirley Williams's marriage can certainly be described as the worst disappointment of her life, and for a time she even considered giving up active politics in the hope of pulling it together again; but her husband rejected this proposal, either because he believed it was made with the half-hearted will of despair, or because he knew it would eventually lead to despair. There are undoubtedly times at which the telling point of the division between dependent and expansive needs emerges in the marriage, while the children look happily after themselves, and thrive in the arrangements made by a busy, professional mother. Marriage may involve a continuing closeness, or may break apart because the closeness does not persist, and we may not be as sufficiently attuned to our husband's needs as we are to our children's. The two problems, the two sets of demands, are often linked in various ways, but they are also different. People have all sorts of different problems within a marriage, but the problems of mothers in regard to their children are far more homogeneous. There is, alas, some truth to the notion of a maternal personality: it is not because women are shallow that they communicate so well with other women, but because they do have a deep sense of a shared experience as mothers, or as potential mothers.

And that is why, when a woman seems to have no problems in balancing her life, we can learn nothing from her. Magazine articles abound on how to manage everything – family, work, friends, hobbies – but these articles, showing how women have it 'all buttoned up', alienate other women rather than stimulate them because women know they will face problems within themselves. Yet there is no harm, I suppose, in looking at one superwoman – the Prime Minister Margaret Thatcher. She is far removed from the tradition of women who manage well with their children because they hardly ever see them, paying only state visits to the nursery while the nanny takes all the rough and tumble. Margaret Thatcher never used a nanny, but instead relied upon her mother, who lived nearby. Before she was married she had enrolled as a student at Lincoln's Inn. Law had always appealed to her, even though she had read chemistry at Oxford. She married, and then two years later, in 1953, gave birth to twins, Mark and Carol, her only children. Four months after they were born she took her bar finals, and qualified. 'I thought that if I didn't do something quite definite then there was a real possibility that I'd never return to work again, so I entered my name for the bar finals. That was really an effort of will because I felt that unless I made it, I would just tend to give it all up and therefore it was almost a challenge to really get stuck into it.' What Mrs Thatcher describes so well here is the initial threat that motherhood brings to what one has previously known as oneself. Over and over again I found women who felt compelled to prove themselves as soon as their baby was born. They had to prove that they could still function as working people, that they could still use their minds, that they could still concentrate on something other than a baby's cries, that they retained sufficient self-assurance to face the world, and to compete in it. This desperate determination was not unnecessary. Many people speak of the isolation of a new mother, but her greatest isolation is from herself, from what she wants herself to be, what she has previously assumed she can be. There are many women who embrace their new maternal self, and happily reorder their priorities. There are women who give up work, after trying for a time to return as a working mother, because they are unexpectedly satisfied by their children, and find they place an unexpected value on raising them themselves, but there are also many women who are confused and depressed and anxious at the unexpected feelings and the shifting emphases. I know women who have had children when they think their doctorate thesis is under control, only to find, when they have a baby, that they no longer have any sense of intellectual direction. The thesis may drag on for years, until it dies on the shelf. Jane Lazarre, the novelist and author of *The Mother Knot,* describes how the books seemed to gather dust on her desk, how they stared at her strangely, no longer able to say anything to her. Previous ambitions became a mockery, and were evident only in her amazed dejection at what she had become. Jane Lazarre eventually emerged from this self-alienation, this dejection, as do many others. But in so far as advice makes any sense in an area frought with individual feelings and needs and circumstances, it does seem advisable to do what Margaret Thatcher did – to make a stand in one's own right as soon as possible, to assume one will continue to need the same exercise of talent and skill one's pre-maternal self required. And then, in time, there will probably be a backsliding, when one wants to give up a little of the effort, and to be closer to one's children. This is not easy, because most careers are difficult to moderate and simultaneously maintain. But women who do this, or attempt this, have the advantage of a sense of success – that of being true to their expansive needs while they become bound to that fragile and demanding and overpowering being – their child.

Mrs Thatcher seems far removed from any threat to self-assurance. She strikes me as someone whom it would be impossible to psychoanalyse, for example, simply because her conscious self is her total self. Yet when she reflects upon her early years of mothering she sounds ordinary enough. 'I worried all the time and of course ninety per cent of the time you worry about things that don't happen – but you still worry! There are times when you think you're never going to get any real sleep again. But suddenly you're through it all . . . ' She is still criticised because of her children – what their activities imply in terms of her position as Prime Minister, and all the attention that goes with being a public figure. Children, at any time in one's life,

157

can call forth the attention and worry one thought one had left behind. Jean Floud, the president of a Cambridge college, thought the worst was over when, as a widow and an academic, she raised two children on her own; but then, in their late teens, they exhibited that dreadful type of adolescent behaviour which crushes all one's self-confidence as a mother, and forces one back to the maternal drawing board. But Margaret Thatcher will never be seriously threatened, and never has been seriously threatened, by the demands of her children, and by her demands upon them. She follows the Hennig–Jardim pattern of a successful woman – she is from a small family, and a family of daughters only; she was closer to her father than to her mother, and her father passed his ambition onto her. Along with his ambition he instilled in her the notion that success alone is admissible. 'I can't' or 'it's too difficult' were remarks he would ignore. It was a tall order, but Margaret Thatcher was obviously up to it. There is, however, room in the world for many things, and there is room not only for failure as a superwoman, but also for sympathy with such failure, and for appreciation of the sensitivity and uncertainty that may make way for such failure. As we groom the next generation of women for success as mothers and professionals, let us also help them see what they need not expect of themselves.

10
Fitting It In – Part Timers and Late Bloomers

Is Mothering A Part-time Job?

Mothering, the feminists of the 1970s noted, is not a full-time job. Women who work in the home are underemployed. They therefore fill their day with useless tasks. They are a prey to advertisers' encouragements to make their floors and windows extra shiny, and to brood over the whiteness of their laundry. These concerns, with other equally meaningless rituals, such as coffee mornings and chauffeuring children to friends and lessons, break up their time into meaningless fragments. They find themselves very busy, but the activity is a fiction, and when they stop to think, they consider their inner emptiness. 'Is this all?' Betty Friedan asked between making the peanut butter sandwiches and waiting for the picnic to begin. This question, 'the

159

question that had no name' because women were not expected to ask it, formed the basis for her book *The Feminine
Mystique*. Women's lives seemed virtually empty, and the
mystique tried to keep this emptiness from them.

Mothering was seen as only a part-time job. Therefore
women could mother and work. Did not African women
work in the fields with their babies in slings, while their
toddlers played beside them? Did not the pioneer women of
America work alongside their husbands while they tended
the children? And in the era before household gadgetry, did
not the children stay at home with the mother while she
worked at home, rather than her staying home with the
children? In modern Western society, man had sabotaged
the workplace and made it unsuitable for women. If women
were allowed to bring their children to work, they would be
able to work. A young MP brought her infant to the House
of Commons, and fed him on demand. In women's small
businesses, children crawled in the reception room. But it
was a limited triumph, just as the truth in what was said,
was limited.

Children are at times part-time work in that one can be
doing something else while looking after them. But they are
adept demanders, and extremely skilled at destroying an
adult's concentration. An infant may be content to be held
while the mother does physical labour – the infant will
then be entertained by the movement – and toddlers or
young children may be content to play while their mothers
work, but they will also have to be supervised, and protected from adult tools of labour. Sometimes mothering is
like being a caretaker – someone has to be there 'in case',
and someone has to be on the lookout for danger. It is
guard duty – a job which does not involve constant action,
but which should involve continuous attention, or readiness
to attend. So the child is nearby, and while the mother is
working he may get up to his own mischief, or may impede her work by 'helping' her. This help may extend the
labour of even the simplest household tasks. Working
with a child at hand is very different from working as we
normally think of it.

There are good reasons for not taking children to work, but if a mother's job is only a very small job, then she could perhaps work at home, where the child can be with his or her own toys and playmates. If the child cannot successfully be brought to the workplace, then the workplace can be brought home – as indeed it once was. For at one time the home was the centre of work, and tasks were shared between husband and wife and any other relatives who happened to be living within the family home. Farming chores and textile production were done in the home, as well as all the tasks which made the home viable – food production, storage, furniture and clothes making. With industrialisation the place of work moved to the factory and away from the home, and the family could not share the work in the same way. Eventually laws prohibited children from working in the factories, and therefore the women had to be at home too, to look after the children; the tasks which were once shared in the home now fell to the mother alone, though the jobs at home were somewhat changed because the money brought home by the factory worker was used to purchase goods which had once been home produced. These goods could be produced so much more efficiently in factories that there was no longer any point in home production. Now that industrialisation has isolated the home from the workplace and made the home a centre for leisure rather than work, could we not bring work to the home and have our time with our children while we work?

Homework

The advantages of working at home are clear. We do not have to change our way of life. We do not have to ask our families to reassess their claims on us. We maintain our domestic control, and we remain as the centre of our family's domestic life. With the proliferation of computers and lightweight machinery there are more and more opportunities for working at home. But the dangers of homework, and the tendency to exploit women who work at home are such that Lesley Garner, in her recent book *How to Survive as a*

Working Mother, declares that no woman in any circumstances should fall into the 'trap' of homework. Garner sees it as exploitation at its most degrading and depressing – and it is sexist exploitation because it is almost entirely women who suffer from it. In Britain there are a quarter of a million homeworkers, and they earn about a quarter of the average earnings for *women* in employment outside the home. Moreover, women who work at home may be endangering their children by installing machinery in their living rooms. Garner is adamant that homework should be avoided.

Why then is it so popular? Are the women who work at home simply too timid to make the break into the 'real' working world? Are they victims of exploitation? Or are they able, by working at home, to order their lives as they would like? Is this a viable way of combining their various needs, in a society not quite prepared for women's various needs?

In the United States homework, though it exists and is often used, is also often illegal, not because laws sought to protect women, but because they sought to protect children from labour abuse. They have, as a side effect, prohibitions against various kinds of adult work in the home. A Congressional committee was set up to investigate infringements on laws prohibiting homework, and Kathy Hobart went to New York to testify before the committee. Hobart lives in Vermont, in a rural area in which child care is virtually unavailable, and from which commuting costs would be high indeed. She runs a knitting business at her home, producing beautiful machine-knit, hand-finished garments that sell in Bloomingdale's for about $200. This is a typical cottage industry – the extension of a domestic occupation into an industry involving professional suppliers and retailers. It is a typically feminine occupation, too, but hardly to be demeaned for that. Many women find knitting and sewing extremely satisfying, and many find it difficult to admit to, or to give in to the pleasure it brings. Freud noticed that sewing, knitting and plaiting and weaving were activities at which women were particularly adept, and he concluded that these skills were developed in response to penis envy. Women weaved and plaited as a desire to arrange their pubic hair in decorative ways which would disguise their 'malformed' or 'castrated' genitals. One could just as well consider them – if they are 'really' weaving and plaiting pubic hair – to be celebrating the place of birth. Freud never considered that the pleasure of mothering was primary, and not derived from something such as the desire for a penis or the desire to be a man. But since this area of psychoanalytic explanation is wild speculation and a show for people's fantasies and prejudices, we can leave it behind. There probably are bioevolutionary reasons for this skill being more common in (but not exclusive to) women.[1] But if such work is done in a factory, women feel alienated from it. They do not choose which garments or patterns to make. The activity is no longer creative, and the work on it no longer provides that healing concentration of an individual effort. We can see a testimony to women's pleasure in such work as the American quilts, and the splendid use of colour and pattern employed by the Amish women (who were forbidden the use of printed materials, but who made magnificent decorations within the permitted limits); quilt-making has also become a cottage industry. Such activities take on a totally different meaning when they are done in factories, but can retain a comparable meaning when they are done at home, according to one's own designs, even if they are now done as a business. Women who are able to do such work do not necessarily fall into a trap, and they are not necessarily exploited. Even if their pay is low, they may come out ahead because they do not have to pay child-care and transport costs.

Another profession women have been able to pursue at home is that of a writer. Some years ago it was usually pointed out that the best women novelists and poets did not have children – Jane Austen, George Eliot, Emily Dickinson – but Mrs Gaskell, who started to write to relieve her grief over the death of a son, is more widely in favour now, and the majority of women writing today do have children. Margaret Drabble described her unexpected passion for her own children, as well as the hours of worry, but these did not deplete her creative urge or energy, and now that her three children are older, and able to entertain themselves, she often works alongside them, retiring to her bedroom while they take over the sitting room. Mary Gordon arranges for her very young daughter to be cared for in the morning when she works. Although she feels herself to be totally enamoured of her child, and would find it extremely difficult to leave the child all day, even though she would also find it extremely difficult not to work, she is able to accept 'part-time' work as thoroughly satisfactory. But the real trump is that for a novelist, a morning's work, which would for most other professions be part time, is usually full time. From Thomas Mann to John Updike, male novelists, too, have chosen to work a few hours each morning as the best way of retaining a fresh and continuing imagination. The novelist who is also a mother may seem to have it all, because she has a full-time job which still allows her to have half the day with her children.

That these lucky cases are so rare, and limited to a highly specific type of talent, speaks for the general difficulty of finding a happy balance. And such cases of mothers as writers do not guarantee a good balance, either. Susan Hill, who had remarkable success as a young novelist, found, after the birth of her son, that she simply did not want to write another novel, and moreover, she did not want to want to write one. The drain on her concentration demanded by a novel set her apart from life. Her infant son kept her geared to life. It is the old cliché of motherhood replacing the need for other creative outlets, but in Hill's case it was hardly this simple. Anyone who knew her believed that she would one day soon write another novel (which she has) no matter how seriously she protested that she was glad not to write. Her brief non-novel-writing years were little more than a breathing space. Being in the grip of a novel one is writing is exhausting, and yet if one is geared to writing novels, one can feel lost when outside such a grip. The birth of her son gave Hill the new knowledge that she could live happily without always thinking about what she would be writing next, without always wondering how this or that in her life could be used in a novel. The discovery of the satisfactions of motherhood was startling and overwhelming and total – but not for long. Her child gave her 'everything', but we can never expect 'everything' to go far enough.

Working at home can be ideal, but clearly it can also be a nuisance. A mother may work at home to avoid complicated or costly child-care arrangements, but she will then find that her work time is cut into by an ill child, or by a baby whose sleep routine is changing. But I have been impressed by the amount a mother can get done in between her children's demands. Mary Hoffman, the journalist and children's writer, has three young daughters, and her only help with them is from a minder of her youngest daughter – and that minder works only two hours each weekday. She is tremendously prolific, however, and sustains her output by thinking about what she has written, what she is going to write, throughout the day. This gives her 'something to do' while she is 'underemployed' as a mother – and there is no doubt that thinking about one's work, and thinking about it in a positive way, can raise one's spirits while dealing with tasks that do not always demand one's full attention or provide sufficient mental stimulus. In the case of women who work with their hands, they learn to pick up their work at every opportunity, making use of five minutes here and there. A children's television programme can bless them with half an hour's work, and they can often turn to this work in the evening, when a writer tends to be too tired to concentrate.

But working at home is also fraught with problems. There are more interruptions, and people are slow to believe that you are working seriously. An aura of success should help in such cases, though people in one's domestic setting tend to be most difficult to impress. Mary Hoffman's most persistent caller during working hours is her mother-in-law, who cannot take in the fact that she should not be disturbed. And I'm sure children are no better. I remember knocking on the closed door of my mother's study as she was preparing for her specialist exams in ophthalmology. 'Is it important?' she demanded. I considered the matter and replied, 'Yes.' The ribbon on one of my stuffed animals had come undone, and it was a beautiful bow. I wanted it retied before the creases were lost, by which time it would be impossible to retrace the original bow.

In an office, too, one is uselessly interrupted, but the interruption of one's colleagues tends to be accepted as part of work, in a way domestic interruptions are not. In fact, working at home can be a disadvantage because it does not provide interruptions from the domestic environment. It does not provide an opportunity to make friends in a non-domestic setting. It does not provide the reinforcement of change, and the relief of getting away from the home. 'I've realised what a nice person I am', one woman reported. She had returned to an office after trying to work at home for five years. 'I've discovered that I do not have to shout at everyone in order to be heard, and I don't feel I'm fighting to have my work recognised.' On the other hand, relationships at work are not always supportive, and one university lecturer said that her colleagues made her realise how nice her children were.

Working at home, if it is not part time (in terms of hours, if not in terms of output) is clearly impossible, and part-time work appeals to mothers for all sorts of reasons. The reasons are obvious – they have time and energy for both their work and their families. The extra stimulus they get from work, the sense of expansion and interest and confidence, has a better chance of doing the family some good, or at least providing the family with some enjoyment, whereas the mother who works full time may consider herself a better or more interesting person because of her job, but may be too tired or distracted to share herself with her family. Also, part-time work tends to be more flexible, so that one can more easily accommodate an ill or disturbed child. It has advantages because we want to give ourselves to others, too. But part-time work can mean that we have to take a less interesting or less influential job. Apart from writers and artists, there are no truly successful part-time women workers. Some women do have very good part-time jobs, but the best jobs are only part time in name. Dorothy Hahn is Bursar of Newnham College, Cambridge – a prestigious and challenging and influential job – and initially it was considered part time, but there is no way she could do that job adequately, let alone well, as a half-time job. And every other interesting job I know of, which is labelled part-time, in fact demands full-time work.

Job-sharing

There are attempts to change this, and one such attempt involves the procedure called job-sharing. A person (who is almost certainly female) finds a 'twin', that is, someone whose qualifications and skills and ideas match hers well enough to create a single working personality. Alternatively, one can find someone to complement one's skills – a civil servant who is strong on political issues may choose as a twin someone who is strong on economics. This is a practice which has been accepted, even by government bureaucracies, but it does make life more complicated for the employer – are there two pension schemes, two sets of family insurance for one job? In some professions there are other difficulties. In law, for example, one twin could be assigned only one client – a client could not have half of each twin's time, because nothing could come together well enough. Also, the job couple I knew best, who worked in the US Treasury, found that they spent a good deal of time conferring on what had been done and what was yet to be done – so much time that they calculated they worked at least three-quarter time, not half time. So it is another example where an interesting part-time job may well be a full-time job in disguise. With rising unemployment, this practice is slow to expand because an employer will not choose someone, or some couple, to fill a vacancy when he faces problems with that couple he does not have to face with a single applicant.

Other attempts have been made, and are being made, by married couples to share child responsibility and financial responsibility equally. Both parents have part-time jobs, and both look after the children. But this can fall down very easily, simply because it is difficult for either parent, let alone both parents, to get good part-time jobs. The most successful cases of shared parenting I found were among divorced couples. 'When we were married', Pat Langerman, a Georgetown University professor, told me, 'my husband's work came between him and his son. But now we are divorced, he has to spend his own time with his son if he is going to see him at all. He can't be around working, while I pick up the tab. If he is with the boy he has to be the single parent. Even temporarily that's a change. So I get every other weekend absolutely free. I can count on that time.' And along with the shared parenting which often comes with divorce (as opposed to parenting together, which often means that the father's time with the children is also the mother's time, but the mother's time is not necessarily the father's time, too), can come financial sharing, in that the father contributes to the children's costs, but not to the mother's, although the mother does not have to carry the burden, as do many fathers, of supporting the entire family. Where child support payments tend to go wrong, a father's interest in his children tends to go wrong, too, but when the father continues to see himself as father, and to value the involvement implied, divorce can result in more equal shares of parenthood.

Part Time – Do the Children Notice?

Most working mothers I spoke to would have been happier working less, and spending more time with their children, but they often do not do this because their careers would have to change radically. But what about the children? Are they happier with part-time working mothers? Most of them would say, 'Yes.' And we can see how a toddler would be glad to have more time – not that any amount of time is ever enough for a toddler! – with his or her mother. Older children would like the company, and teenagers would like to ease the burden on domestic duties. But all of us cope very well with less than our first preferences. The question is whether part-time work makes a difference. When people worry about the effects of maternal employment on children they seldom distinguish between part-time and full-time employment. When Bowlby's report was published in the 1940s[2] the notion of maternal deprivation was like the scare of an epidemic. Women wrote to magazines asking for expert advice on whether it was safe to leave their children for a few hours now and then. And followers of Bowlby today, and there are many of them in the field of child psychology, kindly tell mothers that it is all right for them to have a little time away from their children. But how much is a little? An eight-hour working day? Or a four-hour working day? Or an hour's shopping? Bowlby himself looked at what anyone would consider long-term absences. He considered days and weeks, and days and weeks not at home, among siblings and other relatives, but in hospitals or orphanages. How could we measure or judge the effects of various separation times, without just guessing?

Recently someone did study the differences between infants with part-time and full-time working mothers.[3] The study was geared to the attachment capacities of such infants – and this is the most relevant point, because it is in regard to attachment capacities that Bowlby's studies made people worry. Children deprived of their mothers never develop the confidence and assurance in themselves and others which allow them to look to others for comfort, confirmation, affection. They never develop what Eric Erikson calls 'basic trust',[4] the belief that others can take one's interests to heart, that other people can endorse one's self-image and self-esteem. Having been deprived as infants of a mother's love and admiration, they have no love for themselves and no love to give to others. Therefore, we have the notion of 'good enough mother' from another child psychologist, D. Winnicott, a notion I find patronising – as though to say, 'There, there, you're doing fine, even though you're not perfect' – but it underlines the idea that a mother who rears a nonpsychotic child, or a child who, as an adult, is capable of forming attachments to others, has done her job. The assumption that this is the mother's task may also be thought patronising, but we must allow this type of patronage, even though it smells of male chauvinism, simply because the assumption is generally true. So how much time – in so far as good mothering depends upon time – influences the capacities of the child to form attachments? We understand from Bowlby's studies that, over a period of a few weeks, in institutional surroundings, a child, deprived of his or her mother (and father and grandmother), will go through three stages – first of protest at her absence, then of despair at finding her, then of detachment so that even when the mother returns, the child will seem to have lost a sense of meaning in the attachment, and will not respond, or will respond negatively, to the mother. But what about the cases of separation we are more familiar with – cases in which the mother leaves for a few hours, or a full working day? Pamela Schwartz tried to find out. She selected her sample of children from intact middle-class homes, so the meaning of her studies may be limited, but this sample had the advantage of eliminating other factors – such as the possible pressures of single parenting, or the stress involved when one parent abandons the family, or the complications of extreme poverty, or the ease of wealth, which can engage long-term nannies. It had previously been noticed that an infant who is distressed, but normal, can obtain comfort and reassurance from its mother – even when the distress is caused by the mother's absence. This is a thoroughly commonplace occurrence – the infant clinging to the mother and being comforted by her and forgetting fears in her embrace – but there is a wide variation in the quickness with which an infant can be comforted. Pamela Schwartz set up an experiment in which the child was introduced to the experimenter with the mother. The mother remained while the child explored the surroundings and made contact with the experimenter. Then the mother left the room. She returned, left again, and returned. The focus of the test was to see how long it took for the infant to reestablish a comforting relationship with her.

There were various responses, some very negative, but considered well within normal limits. Some infants, when reunited with their mothers, avoided them. Others displayed clearer signs of distress, such as crying or throwing tantrums while resisting the physical comfort the mother offered. Such behaviour is usually interpreted as punishing the mother for abandoning the child – the child who resists the mother's advances is expressing anger directly, and the child who simply ignores the mother is expressing anger indirectly. Both types of response were considered normal – but those infants who were not able to obtain comfort from their mother and reestablish a reassuring bond with her by the end of the session, were considered abnormal, or 'non-normatively attached'. This would be precisely what those who are against working mothers would look for. The study showed that infants who were in day care displayed more avoidant behaviour towards the mother, and were slower to reestablish a comforting bond with her, and were sometimes unable to do this within the experimental session, in contrast to infants who were at home with their mothers all day – but these differences were accounted for only by those who attended day care full time. There were no differences between those infants who attended day care part time and those who were home all day with their mothers. The difficulties a child had in coping with a mother's absence were not cumulative – that is, they did not start at zero, with the mother home all day, and progress to midpoint when the mother worked half time, and then peak when the mother worked full time. There simply was no difference to be found between the responses of infants at home all day with their mothers and infants who were separated from their mothers for half the day.

Why is this? Is it because women who work part time are able to put in that quality time, that special time for attention and stimulation and responsiveness, for which a full-time working mother may simply be too tired? Is it because full-time working mothers, when at home, usually find it necessary to attend to household responsibilities and to keeping things going, rather than to their children's entertainment? Is it because the full-time working mother's guilt poisons her relationship with her child, so that something goes wrong with her attempts at making quality time? Is she herself ambivalent? And, in any case, what do the results of Schwartz's study mean? Do they do more than measure an infant's immediate response? Have they any wider implications?

It is not clear that an infant's ambivalence towards the mother, and the infant's slowness to overcome the negative side of the ambivalence, have any bearing upon the child's personality and the adult's capacity to form emotional attachments. Some psychologists have observed that the type of behaviour an infant displays towards the mother, when he is reunited with the mother, is stable over time – but perhaps this is because it is related to the mother's responsiveness to the infant in the first year of life, rather than to the mother's work schedule. There may be some evidence, too, that there is a relation between the behaviour exhibited by the infant towards the mother and the development of later social skills, that the infant who is reluctant to trust the mother is the child who is slow to develop socially. All these are questions which every working mother faces. And all these are questions which raise anxiety rather than answers, because there are too many variables to allow for general answers.

Part Time and the Sting of Competition

Many feminists have seen the advantages of part-time work, and have suggested that work situations and career patterns should become more flexible. The real sore point to any compromise in working time, however, is that as long as women want to compete with men, or to keep pace in their careers with men, they will be held back if they do not work the hours men do. Perhaps they will simply have to accept that they cannot compete with men, if they want to retain those important qualities which urge them to mother their children. And perhaps men will come to value similar qualities in themselves. There is some evidence of a change among young men. They want to spend more time with their families, and to have more time for themselves.[5] But those who are most ambitious will not give way to these quieter aims, and women who want to be 'as good as' these men will have difficulty because, in mothers, those aims towards caring for others do not speak so quietly.

The same problem about competing with others who work more faces women who take time away from work to rear their children. In favourable and fair work conditions, jobs may be held during an extended maternity leave, but people who are not at work lose the experience that others who stay at work gain. They miss out on the development of new skills, on the formation of current contacts. There is no way someone who is out of the workplace for a significant period can remain a serious competitor with those who remain. Work advancement cannot be made 'fair' or equal for women in high pressure, upwardly-mobile careers, who take off time for their children. Even in the professions, which may not be as obviously competitive as certain businesses, a woman who takes time off has a tremendous amount of catching up to do. One doctor who worked part time for three years when she had two children, found that when her youngest son was in school, the programme she had been following – that of building up a specialty in diabetes at a nearby hospital – was not continued. She could either continue to work one day a week and, in fourteen years, be ready to apply for a consultancy – by which time she would be competing with far younger people – or she could change direction and become a general practitioner. She opted for the latter, which was a more viable alternative, but she was still, when she finished her training and was ready to apply to various practices, competing with younger people. Nor was she, because her family was settled, as mobile as a young man, who could move near any desirable practice. A woman who makes allowances for her family cannot expect to succeed as one who does not. Positive discrimination for women who interrupt their working lives to care for their children is highly unlikely, and without it the woman who does take off time for her children will be held back at work.

The Empty Nest

But motherhood is not forever – not, at any rate, the intensive stages which do require an awful lot of time and energy. The feminists of fifteen years ago were surprised and astounded to view schoolgirls' accounts of their lives. They finished school or university or college, and then got married, had children, raised their children to school age – and the next time a vision of their lives featured was as grandmothers, taking care of their daughters' children. A long expanse of their adult lives – when they did not have to be on hand for their children – was a blank.

There is then another way in which a woman could have a part-time career. She could have a career for part of her life – a full-time career when her children are no longer small. Many women who are highly conservative in their assessment of a mother's task, are proud career women in their forties and fifties, when their children are grown. 'The years of raising children are so short', remarked an executive in the cosmetics firm Revlon. 'I don't see why these women are in such a hurry.' There are indeed many success stories of women who, with no previous experience, build up careers they have started in middle age. Often the careers start as work they can do at home – the Revlon executive began as an assistant editor of Revlon's advertising. She provided something like 'the ordinary woman's response' to various advertising slogans and images. The novelist again has a good chance as a woman, because she is not expected to earn money straight away, and because her tools and her material can be found in any home. Judith Guest, author of the best-seller *Ordinary People*, reports that she was truly satisfied with her life as a suburban housewife before she started writing, but that when her youngest child started school, she had nothing to do, and so she wrote. Given that she wrote as she did, it is hard to believe she was perfectly satisfied, in that she exposes great gaps of feeling within that life, but she also suggests that they can be solved and that there is a place for reparation and understanding, as well as for the terrors of self-knowledge and self-defeat. And whatever the secret reservations which she harboured and brooded upon along the way, she devoted herself to being a wife and mother until the natural break came when her devotions were not in constant demand.

Gender Characteristics Change in Middle Age

It is often said that as women become older, they become more 'masculine' – that is, more aggressive, more self-centred, more keen on defining a goal for themselves – and that men become more 'feminine' – that is, they care more about forming and maintaining relationships, value the expression of warmth, and need to be loved – as they grow older.[6] In so far as a woman's nurturing impulses are geared specifically to the raising of children, this pattern has a clear logic. The children stimulate the mother's attachment and involvement when they need it – which may in turn stimulate the man to become the aggressive protector. But when the children are adults and no longer need a child's care and protection, the parents are free to develop other characteristics and along with them, other interests. As the child's influence upon gender traits fades, the woman may become more self-interested and self-involved. Selfishness no longer harms those in her charge.

Is it not then a natural division of life, for a woman to devote her years as a young adult to bearing and rearing children, and her middle and late years to a career? This surely is one good way of having it all, while denying other people close to one nothing. Many women swear by it. Most of us know women who keep their talents ticking silently away, until they have the time to develop them. I first met Maggie Scarf, author of *Unfinished Business* – that powerful and popular book on depression and women – when her three children were nine, twelve and sixteen. They still formed the focus of her time, but she was obviously aware of their growing independence, and of her changing role, and was searching for a way to harness her obvious talents. She had done some professional writing, and she tried to launch into a novel, but it was somehow not right for her. Eventually she began to write as a journalist on scientific subjects, and her career was away and clear. But she had already been preparing herself, unaware, for this career, or one like it. She had been particularly receptive to certain ideas and feelings. She had been particularly interested in general undercurrents of individual lives, and the ways in which women tried to improve or to cope with their lives. She had found her career in the best possible way – she had discovered that her interests did after all have a focus, and that she had for years been preparing herself for an in-depth study of certain psychological themes. An impression here, an understanding gained there, were hoarded over years, or perhaps written down in one of those precious quiet hours she used to make for herself, when everyone was asleep, or happened to be out. 'I'm glad I stayed home with my children', she said, 'because it doesn't seem that long when they were little, and at home with me.' Her conclusion is in keeping with the conclusions in her book. Women, she believes, value human attachment, and need to be loved, to be needed, by others; they need to nurture others, and they naturally respond more to others' needs than do men. A woman's greater proneness to depression is due to these facts: depression is triggered by a loss, and the loss is that of an important relationship, which reverberates throughout her psyche because all relationships are reminiscent of one another and the loss of one will stir memories of previous unresolved relationships.

Late Bloomers Fail To See How They Have Changed

This was a strange book, based as it was on a very limited and even outdated view of depression, and looking as it did only at women, while none the less setting out to show that women were different from men. Scarf claimed that men became depressed about not 'making it', not succeeding, whereas women became depressed about not maintaining relationships. But what does success mean to a man? Does success not bear with it the need to prove oneself, or to earn love? And in women, where does that excessive dependence upon relationships come from? Is it not in part from an emptiness, a lack of self-direction, a sense that one is too inexperienced to cope alone? Women and men are different, but there are important points in which all people meet. Because they are different, however, special cases, biased views, can always gain a foothold. Maggie Scarf's theory is ultimately biased, but it became popular because it spoke to women's own biases about themselves, and it flattered their weaknesses, all the while damaging them by putting them more at sea in regard to their own needs. Yes, they need to nurture, and they need to form and maintain relationships, but they also need independence and the self-confidence which goes with independence, and the self-respect and freedom that goes with having goals outside, or, rather, alongside the people to whom they are close. Scarf showed this, but then denied it. She spoke of her early days as a mother, isolated in her husband's academic environment, the threatening silences that encompassed her and her infant. But what of this? Women need others, and so they put themselves in danger by valuing a career above a relationship, claims Scarf.

There is only one woman in Scarf's large book who is seriously committed to a career, and that woman suffers not from commonplace depression, but from a manic-depressive syndrome, which is not differently distributed among men and women. Many of the other women who are depressed may be depressed because they are lost within themselves, and turn to others to give them what others cannot give. 'My children give me everything', we hear over and over again, and it is true in that children give one all they could possibly give — all one needs from them, but one needs other things as well. The overwhelming involvement a new mother has in her infant may create a life-long bond, but both the bond and the concentrated involvement change, and give way to other things. And even before they give way to adult independence, even before a woman confronts an 'empty nest', she confronts herself, and her need to develop, to meet challenges, to exhibit mastery within the framework of her society. Some women who are very lucky are still able to do this, even if they do not seriously begin such work until middle age – but this is playing with fire. It is playing with fire because women are then in danger of losing touch with their talents, of losing any confidence that they can develop, and they are in danger of becoming excessively dependent upon others, so that their response to the loss of relationship, or the diminishment of a relationship's intensity, is then, according to Scarf's pattern, depression.

Late bloomers are the survivors of the traditional institution of motherhood, but simply because there are survivors does not mean that it is an institution which should not change. And it is changing – its changes mark the most significant change in our society today. It is changing so much that we are sometimes puzzled by the way it remains constant. We have to make sense of its constancy and its change, and we have to understand what we are doing as we honour it, or deviate from it. What risks do we take with ourselves and our children? We have to change it to suit our needs, because we have to have confidence that children were meant to have people as mothers.

11
Looking Ahead

We have seen young women, the daughters of working mothers, who do not want to go out to work when their children are small. We have seen young women who shun the term 'feminist' because of its hostile, militant associations. But the working mothers of today have none the less had their effect. Young women, by and large, want what these women want, because the generations of adult women have taught them to acknowledge their needs. Dr Carol Travis, a social psychologist, recently conducted a survey of 10 000 women between the ages of seventeen and thirty (though 87 per cent were under twenty-five) and found that only 2 per cent of the sample did not intend to work at all. These women, it seemed, understood that they would have to be self-supporting, or significant contributors to family income, during some period of their lives. But these young women also wanted to have children, and not merely to have them, but to stay at home with them for two to six years – this is what 60 per cent planned to do. The same number planned to earn $25 000 or above at the peak of their careers – a salary that in fact is earned by only 2 per cent of working women today. These expectations may seem laughably high – but they are not much higher than those of men in the US, for whom the average salary is not much less than $25 000 a year, and most of whom have children. Yet they do not stay at home with the children, as these young women want to do.

Continued rapid growth in the number of working women will probably be the most significant change in the workforce this century. Not only will more women work, but they will work for longer, and bring more qualifications with them. But as more women work, will they achieve gains in salary and status – as young women clearly believe they will? Youthful expectations have some influence over the future, but the simple fact that these expectations are widely shared may prevent many women from realising them. For as more women work, they will be in competition with one another, and they will be in competition with men, because the economy, to say the least, is not expanding as quickly as the number of working people is growing.

Women, in general, are not good at competing with men for jobs, or for salaries. In America the national ratio of women's to men's earnings is 59 cents to every dollar (though the black woman earns only 47 cents to every white male dollar earned) and top professional women earn about 73 per cent of what male professionals earn. The situation, both in Europe and America, is getting worse, not better. Not only has the gap between the wages of women and men widened, but, what is more worrying, the old division between good work and mediocre work, promising careers and dead-end jobs, remains a division between men's work and women's work. According to the latest Census Bureau report, nearly 80 per cent of women are still in clerical, sales, service, technical, factory or plant jobs. Lawyers, judges and engineers account for less than 1 per cent of all employed women. Sexual integration of the workplace is occurring more as a result of males turning to occupations such as nursing, receptionist and telephone operator, than women successfully turning to male spheres of work. The gains women have made are slowing down. While women represented nearly 20 per cent of all employed managers and administrators in 1982 – a rise of 16 per cent since 1970 – that progress has virtually stopped. Women's rights, and women's hopes, are a casualty of the recession.

When I began writing this book I believed that the women I interviewed represented an expanding trend. I believed this because it was true at the time, and because I was, and still am, convinced that women's happiness depends upon such a trend. But it is now clear that we run the considerable risk of having in effect two worlds – one where the minority of women enjoy a greater degree of opportunity, and the other where the majority of women are in low-paid, sex-segregated jobs. The élite, who are able to make good use of some diminishment in bias, generally come from privileged backgrounds. And it is still so difficult to compete with men because women have children, and mother their children; and work patterns are not becoming more flexible nor are day-care places expanding significantly. In Britain and America there are, at present, fewer day-care facilities than there were in 1945, when wartime made women's work truly valued. However, the demand for more places is being picked up by the American market, and some firms are making child care big business, by mass-producing building and equipment along fast food chain lines.

In Britain, however, women will have even less choice. The tax man has never been kind to the mother who needs child care for her work either in Britain or the United States (I have heard it repeatedly said that the working mother in the United States does get tax concessions for child care, but the concessions allowed are laughably small and they depend upon her filing jointly with her husband). Companies in Britain who provide creches for the children of employees have been able to record this as a business expense, and therefore are sometimes willing to subsidise child care. This tremendous benefit for working mothers was unfortunately too flagrant. It is a benefit in kind, the

Inland Revenue has decided, and therefore taxable – that means that the parents will be taxed on the cost of the child care. The full cost of the child care will be added to the monetary value of their income. This will mean, for many women, that they can no longer afford to work, since their bills for child care will go up by about £70 a month. It will be the end of company-attached creches.

The depressing forecasts are just emerging in the public eye, but it seems that the ambitious young women of today, the women now working towards, but not quite embarking upon, their careers, already know this. A year ago I visited Harvard Medical School and spent a few days with six young women in the class who were approaching graduation. In a few months they would be qualified doctors, so it was not surprising that they were self-consciously serious, tediously opinionated, and prepared to save patients not only from the patients themselves but from all other doctors who knew less than they did. These women had embraced their independence – not one of them was married – but they embraced it with such vehemence that it was clear they were not certain about it. They were not going to have children, they declared. They had worked hard to gain admission to medical school – and Harvard Medical School was described as 'impossibly competitive'. They were not prepared to put their achievements under siege – with children, with husbands. At the same time they were remarkably concerned about their appearance, and discussed clothes and make-up and figures and diets with· the same intensity they discussed their forthcoming exams. For whom were they preening themselves? They were friends with their colleagues, but few had had any boyfriends among them. 'They want someone softer', one young woman explained. 'We're too ambitious for them.' And their male colleagues admitted this. 'They think about their work all the time. They always tell us that their work comes first. Always them and their work first. I'm happy to have a wife who works. I expect to have a wife who works. But I don't want to be told all the time that I come second.'

It was clear that these women would not be like this all

their lives. The vehemence was necessary at this stage in their careers, because they knew their determination was threatened by their dependency needs. 'It's not so much sex I need, as physical closeness', one girl told me in private. 'Sometimes when I am studying I just close my eyes and imagine someone stroking my hair. It's not easy to be alone, but the guys around here expect me to support them, and find ways of making their lives easier – and that's what I want from a guy. I'm not going to trade a boyfriend for freedom to work as hard as I want.' In private, too, most of them admitted that perhaps one day they would want a child (they always said 'a child', never 'children', though most women who have one child then go on to have another). But many women have succeeded in having both children and a career, and if any young women were confident about their careers, these women were. Why then did they lack the assurance that they could 'have it all' – career, child and husband?

'The woman always gets stuck with the kid', they explained. 'If anything goes wrong, the woman has to carry the burden.' But these women could take charge of their own lives. They were strong enough and sensible enough to see what was going on, and to make arrangements to protect their interests, like a man. Weren't they?

What these women knew was that the burden of motherhood would come from within, and that they would be left holding the baby because they would respond to the baby more strongly, more immediately than anyone else. These women, who have the privilege of choice – a privilege which after all will not be shared by very many in the new generation of working women – because they have already developed their expansive needs, and developed them in a marketable fashion, and will be able to afford to make their own arrangements for child care, will probably not forego the privileges of motherhood. But already they know their stories will not be easy ones, and already they know that the women who are now living lives like theirs will one day be, cannot offer a simple and straightforward and safe pattern. We must understand that the future for working mothers, who aim for professional success, is still being created, and we are only just beginning to accept what the problems in its creation really are.

Notes and References

Chapter One

1. Horney, Karen, *Neurosis and Human Growth* (New York: W. W. Norton, 1950); and Symonds, Alexandra, 'The Psychodynamics of Expansiveness in Success-Oriented Woman', *The American Journal of Psychoanalysis*, 38 (1978) 195–205.

2. Broverman, Inge K., Broverman, Donald M., Clarkson, Frank E., Rozenkrantz, Paul S., and Vogel, Susan R., 'Sex-role Stereotypes and Clinical Judgments of Mental Health', *Journal of Consulting and Clinical Psychology*, 34:1-7, 1 (1970).

3. Chodorow, Nancy, *The Reproduction of Mothering* (Berkeley: University of California Press, 1978).

4. Symonds, Alexandra, 'Neurotic Dependency in Successful Women', *Journal of the American Academy of Psychoanalysis*, 4, 1 (1976) 95–103.

Chapter Two

1. Pollock, Linda, paper presented to the Historical Society, Churchill College, Cambridge, 'Child-rearing Practices in 17th-century America and Britain', 7 November 1983.

2. Balint, Alice, and Balint, Michael, Benedeck, Theresa, Winnicott, D., 'The Theory of Parent–Infant Relationship', *International Journal of Psycho Analysis*, 41 (1960) 593–4.

3. Paper presented to the conference on Women's Studies in Psychiatric Education, San Francisco, 28 January 1983.

4. Friedan, Betty, *The Second Stage* (New York: Summit Books, 1981).

5. Dowling, Colette, *The Cinderella Complex* (New York: Summit Books, 1981).

6. Rossi, Alice, 'A Biosocial Perspective on Parenting', *Daedelus*, 106, no. 2 (1978) 1–31.

7. Stoller, Robert, 'The "Bedrock" of Masculinity and Femininity: Bisexuality', *Archives of General Psychiatry*, 26 (1972) 207–12.

8. Money, J., 'How Gender Identity is Formed', *Sexual Medicine Today*, December 1976.

9. Mitchell, Juliet, *Psychoanalysis and Feminism* (New York: Pantheon Books, 1974).

10. Maccoby, Eleanor, and Jacklin, Carol, *The Psychology of Sex Differences* (Stanford University Press, 1974).

11. Lever, Janet, 'Sex Differences in the Games Children Play', *Social Problems*, 23 (1976) 478–87.

12. Gilligan, Carol, *In a Different Voice* (Cambridge, Mass.: Harvard University Press, 1982).

Chapter Three

1. The *Sunday Times* Magazine, 'Loneliness', 5 December 1983.

2. Leach, Penelope, *Who Cares? A New Deal for Mothers and their Small Children* (Harmondsworth: Penguin, 1979).

3. Harlow, H.E., Harlow, M.K., Dodsworth, R.O., and Arling, G.L., 'Maternal Behaviour in Rhesus Monkeys Deprived of Mothering and Peer Association in Infants', in Freda Rekelsy (ed.), *Child Development and Behaviour* (New York: Alfred A. Knopf, 1970).

4. Mahler, Margaret, *The Psychological Development of the Human Infant* (New York: Basic Books, 1976).

5. Leach, *Who Cares?*

6. Cf. Rutter, Michael, *Maternal Deprivation Reassessed* (Middx: C. Nicholls & Co., 1972).

7. Hoffman, Lois Waldis, 'The Effects of Maternal Employment on the Academic Attitudes and Performance of School-Aged Children', *School Psychology Review*, 9 (1980) 319–35.

8. Moore, T.W., 'Exclusive Mothering and its Alternatives', *Scandinavian Journal of Psychology*, 16 (1975) 256–73.

9. Moles, Oliver, National Institute of Education, paper presented to conference 25 March 1983, Washington D.C.

Chapter Four

1. Hoffman, Lois Waldis, 'Early Childhood Experiences and Women's Achievement Motives', *J. of Social Issues*, 28(2) (1972) 129–55.

2. Woolf, Virginia, *A Room of One's Own* (London: Hogarth Press, 1929).

3. Horner, Matina, 'Femininity and Successful Achievement: A Basic Inconsistency,' in Bardwick, J.M., Douvan, E., Horner, M.S., and Gutman, D., *Feminine Personality and Conflict* (California: Brooks/Cole, 1972).

4. Simon, J.G., and Feather, N.T., 'Causal Attributions for Success and Failure at University Examinations', *Journal of Educational Psychology*, 64 (1973) 46–56. Jones, E.E., Kanouse, D.E., Kelley, H.H., Nisbett, R.E., Valins, S., and Weiner,

B., *Attribution: Perceiving the Causes of Behaviour* (Morristown, New Jersey: General Learning Press, 1971).

5. Sassen, Georgia, 'Success Anxiety in Women: A Constructivist Interpretation of its Source and its Significance', *Harvard Educational Review*, vol. 50, no. 1 (February 1980).

Chapter Five

1. Weissman, Myrna, and Klerman, Gerald, 'Sex Differences and the Epidemiology of Depression', *Archives of General Psychiatry*, vol. 34 (January 1977) 98–111.

2. Epstein, Seymour and Fenz, Walter, in Gardner Linzey, and Calvin Halls (eds), *Theories of Personality: Primary Sources and Research* (Ann Arbor: University of Michigan, 1979).

3. Radloff, Lenore, 'Sex Differences in Depression', *Sex Roles*, vol. 1, no. 3 (1975) 249–56.

4. Seligman, M., 'Learned Helplessness and Depression', in R. Friedrich and M. Katz (eds), *The Psychology of Depression: Contemporary Theory and Research* (Washington D.C.: US Government Printing House, to be published). Beck, Aaron, T., *Cognitive Therapy and Emotional Disorders* (New York: International Universities Press, 1976).

Chapter Six

1. Stewart, Wendy Ann, 'A Psychosocial Study of the Formation of Early Adult Life Structure in Women', doctoral dissertation (Columbia University, New York, 1976).

2. Levinson, Daniel, *The Seasons of a Man's Life* (New York: Alfred A. Knopf, 1978).

Chapter Eight

1. Fingleton, David, *Kiri* (London: Collins, 1982).

Chapter Nine

1. Hennig, Margaret and Jardim, Anne, *The Managerial Woman* (London: Pan, 1979).

2. Korn/Ferry International, *Profile of Women Senior Executives* (Washington D.C., 1982).

3. Angell, M., 'Juggling the Personal and Professional Life', *Journal of the American Medical Women's Association*, vol. 37 (1982) 64–8.

4. Heins, M., Smock, S., Martindale, L. *et al.*, 'A Profile of the Woman Physician', *Journal of the American Medical Women's Association*, vol. 32 (1977) 421–7.

5. Bolton, Susan, 'Feminism', *New York Times* Magazine, 28 October 1982.

Chapter Ten

1. Rossi, 'Biosocial Perspective on Parenting'.

2. Bowlby, John, *Maternal Care and Mental Health* (Geneva: World Health Organisation, 1952).

3. Schwartz, Pamela, 'Working Mothers of Infants: Conflicts and Coping Strategies', in *Women's Lives*, Centre for Women's Studies (University of Michigan, Ann Arbor, Michigan, 1979).

4. Erikson, E., *Childhood and Society*, 2nd edn (New York: W.W. Norton, 1963).

5. Sheehy, Gail, *Pathfinders* (New York: William Morrow, 1981).

6. Cf. Levinson, *Seasons of a Man's Life*.

Selected Bibliography

Adams, Jane, *Making Good* (New York: Morrow, 1980).

Adams, Jane, *Women on Top* (New York: Morrow, 1978).

Ainsworth, M.D. *et al.*, *Deprivation of Maternal Care: A Reassessment of its Effects* (New York: Schocken Books, 1966).

Akiskal, Hagop S. and William T. McKinney, 'Overview of Recent Research in Depression', *Archives of General Psychiatry*, 32 (March 1975) 285–95.

Austin, Richard, *Lynn Seymour: An Authorised Biography* (London: Angus & Robertson, 1980).

Barber, Dulan, *One-parent Families* (London: Davis-Poynter, 1978).

Bardwick, Judith, 'The Dynamics of Successful People', *New Research on Women* (Ann Arbor: University of Michigan Press, 1981).

Bardwick, Judith, *Psychology of Women* (New York: Harper & Row, 1971).

Bardwick, Judith, *Readings on the Psychology of Women* (New York: Harper & Row, 1972).

Bardwick, Judith *et al.*, *Feminine Personality and Conflict* (California: Brooks/Cole, 1970).

Beck, Aaron T., *Depression: Clinical, Experimental and Theoretical Aspects* (New York: Harper & Row, 1967).

Beck, Aaron T., *Cognitive Therapy and Emotional Disorders* (New York: International University Press, 1976).

Bernard, Jessie, *The Future of Marriage* (New York: World Publishing, 1972).

Bowlby, John, *Attachment and Loss*, vol. 1 (London: Hogarth Press, 1969), vol. 2 (New York: Basic Books, 1973), vol. 3 (London: Hogarth Press and Institute of Psychoanalysis, 1980).

Braslow, Judith B., and Marilyn Heins, 'Women in Medical Education', *New England Journal of Medicine*, 305 (May 1981) 1129–35.

Broverman, Inge, *et al.*, 'Sex Role Stereotypes and Clinical Judgments of Mental

189

Health', *Journal of Consulting and Clinical Psychology*, 34 (February 1970).

Bruner, Jerome, *Under Five in Britain* (London: Grant McIntyre, 1980).

Cahill, Susan (ed.), *Motherhood: A Reader for Men and Women* (New York: Avon Books, 1982).

Cater, Libby A., and Anne Firor Scott, *Women and Men: Changing Roles, Relationships and Perceptions* (New York: Praeger, 1977).

Chesler, Phyllis, *Women and Madness* (London: Allen Lane, 1972).

Chodorow, Nancy, *The Reproduction of Mothering* (Berkeley: University of California Press, 1978).

Curtis, J., *Working Mothers* (New York: Doubleday, 1976).

Dally, Ann, *Inventing Motherhood* (London: Burnett Books, 1982).

de Beauvoir, Simone, *The Second Sex* (Harmondsworth: Penguin, 1972).

Deutsch, Helen, *The Psychology of Women* (New York: Grune and Stratton, 1944).

Dinnerstein, Dorothy, *The Rocking of the Cradle and the Ruling of the World* (London: Souvenir Press, 1976).

Dowling, Colette, *The Cinderella Complex* (New York: Summit Books, 1981).

Epstein, Cynthia Fuchs, *Women's Place, Options and Limits in Professional Careers* (Berkeley: University of California Press, 1970).

Erikson, Erik H., *Childhood and Society*, 2nd edn (New York: W.W. Norton, 1963).

Erikson, Erik H., *Identity, Youth and Crisis* (New York: W.W. Norton, 1968).

Fingleton, David, *Kiri* (London: Collins, 1982).

Fonda, N. and P. Moss, *Mothers in Employment* (London: Brunel University and Thomas Coram Research Unit, 1976).

Freud, Anna and Dorothy Burlingham, *Young Children in Wartime* (London: Allen & Unwin, 1942).

Freud, Anna and Dorothy Burlingham, *Infants Without Families* (London: Allen & Unwin, 1943).

Freud, Sigmund, 'Female Sexuality' in J. Strachey (ed.), *Standard Edition*, vol. 21 (London: Hogarth Press, 1961) pp. 223–43.

Freud, Sigmund, 'Feminity', in J. Strachey (ed.), *Standard Edition*, vol. 22 (London: Hogarth Press, 1964) pp. 112–35.

Friedan, Betty, *The Second Stage* (New York: Summit Books, 1981).

Friedman, Martha, *Overcoming the Fear of Success* (New York: Warner Books, 1980).

Garner, Lesley, *How to Survive as a Working Mother* (Harmondsworth: Penguin, 1982).

Gathorne-Hardy, Jonathan, *The Rise and Fall of the British Nanny* (London: Hodder & Stoughton, 1972).

Gavron, Helen, *The Captive Wife* (Harmondsworth: Penguin, 1968).

Gilligan, Carol, *In a Different Voice* (Cambridge, Mass.: Harvard University Press, 1982).

Gornick, Vivian and Barbara K. Moran (eds), *Women in a Sexist Society* (New York: Basic Books, 1971).

Greer, Germaine, *The Female Eunuch* (London: MacGibbon & Kee, 1970).

Harlow, H.K. and M.K. Harlow 'Learning to Love', *American Scientist*, 54(3) (1966) 244–72.

Heffner, Elaine, *Mothering* (New York: Doubleday, 1978).

Heins, Marilyn, *et al.*, 'Current Status of Women Physicians', *International Journal of Women's Studies*, 1(3) (1978) 297–305.

Heins, Marilyn, *et al.*, 'The Importance of Extra-Family Support on Career Choices of Women', *Personnel and Guidance Journal* (April 1982).

Heins, Marilyn, *et al.*, 'Attitudes of Women and Men Physicians', *American Journal of Public Health*, 69 (11) (1979) 1132–9.

Heins, Marilyn and Jane Thomas, 'Women Medical Students: A New Appraisal', *Journal of the American Medical Association*, 34 (11) (1979) 408–15.

Hoffman, L.W., 'Effects of Maternal Employment on the Child: A Review of the Research', *Developmental Psychology*, 10(2) (1974) 204–28.

Selected Bibliography

Hoffman, L.W., 'The Effects of Maternal Employment on the Academic Attitudes and Performance of School-Aged Children', *School Psychology Review*, 9 (1980) 319–35.

Horner, Matina, 'Fail: Bright Women', *Psychology Today*, 3(6) (1969) 36.

Horner, Matina, 'Toward an Understanding of Achievement Related Conflicts in Women', *Journal of Social Issues* (1972).

Horney, Karen, *Neurosis and Human Growth: The Struggle toward Self Realisation* (New York: W.W. Norton, 1950).

Horney, Karen, *Feminine Psychology* (New York: W.W. Norton, 1967).

Huber, Joan (ed.), *Changing Women in a Changing Society* (University of Chicago Press, 1973).

Janeway, Elizabeth, *Man's World, Woman's Place* (New York, Dell, 1971).

Kinzer, Nora Scott, *Stress and the American Woman* (New York: Ballantine Books, 1980).

Kudsin, Ruth B. (ed.), *Women and Success* (New York: William Morrow, 1974).

Leach, Penelope, *Who Cares? A New Deal for Mothers and their Small Children* (Harmondsworth: Penguin, 1979).

Levinson, Daniel J., *The Seasons of a Man's Life* (New York: Alfred A. Knopf, 1978).

Llewelyn Davies, Margaret (ed.), *Maternity: Letters from Working Women* (London: Virago, 1978).

Maccoby, Eleanor and Carol Nagy Jackson, *The Psychology of Sex Differences* (Stanford: Stanford University Press, 1974).

Mahler, Margaret, *The Psychological Development of the Human Infant* (New York: Basic Books, 1976).

McDonnell, Liz, *Money Matters for Women* (London: Collins in association with the Women's Institute, 1983).

Mead, Margaret, *Male and Female* (New York and London: Morrow, 1949).

Mead, Margaret and Martha Wolfenstein (eds), *Childhood in Contemporary Cultures* (University of Chicago Press, 1955).

Mednick, M.T.S. *et al.*, *Women and Achievement* (New York: Wiley, 1975).

Miller, Jean Baker, *Toward a New Psychology of Women* (Boston: Beacon Press, 1977).

Mitchell, Juliet, *Women's Estate* (Harmondsworth: Penguin, 1971).

Mitchell, Juliet, *Psychoanalysis and Feminism* (London: Allen Lane, 1974).

Money, J., 'How Gender Identity is Formed', *Sexual Medicine Today* (December 1976).

Moulton, Ruth, 'Women with Double Lives', *Journal of Contemporary Psychoanalysis*, 13 (January 1977) 64.

Murray, Tricia, *Margaret Thatcher* (London: W. H. Allen, 1978).

Nadelson, C. *et al.*, 'Success or Failure: Psychotherapeutic Considerations for Women in Conflict', *American Journal of Psychiatry*, 135(9) (1978) 1092–6.

Nadelson, C. *et al.*, 'Psychotherapy Supervision: The Problem of Conflicting Values', *American Journal of Psychotherapy*, 32(2) (1977) 275–83.

Nadelson, C., 'The Psychology of Women: An Overview', paper presented to the American Psychiatric Association conference, Women's Studies in Psychiatric Education (San Francisco, 27 January 1983).

Nadelson, C. and Malkah Notman, *Women, Work and Children* (in press).

O'Reilly, Jane, *The Girl I Left Behind* (New York: Macmillan, 1982).

Pollock, Linda, *Forgotten Children: Parent–Child Relationships from 1500 to 1900* (Cambridge University Press, 1983).

Radloff, Lenore, 'Sex Differences in Depression', *Sex Roles*, 1(3) (1975) 249–65.

Rapoport, R. and R.N. Rapoport, *Duel Career Families Re-examined* (London: Martin Robertson, 1976).

Rich, Adrienne, *Of Woman Born* (London: Virago, 1977).

Rossi, Alice S., 'A Biosocial Perspective on Parenting', *Daedelus*, 106(2) (1977) 1–31.

Rossi, Alice S., 'Life-Span Theories and Women's Lives', *Signs: Journal of Women in Culture and Society*, 6(1) (1980) 4–32.

Rothbart, Mary and Eleanor Maccoby, 'Parents' Differential Reactions to Sons and Daughters', *Journal of Personality and Social Psychology*, 4(3) (1966).

Rutter, Michael, *Maternal Deprivation Reassessed* (Middlesex: C. Nicholls, 1972).

Sassen, Georgia, 'Success Anxiety in Women: A Constructivist Interpretation of its Source and its Significance', *Harvard Educational Review*, 50 (1) (February 1980) 13–24.

Scarf, Maggie, *Unfinished Business: Pressure Points in the Lives of Women* (New York: Doubleday, 1980).

Schaffer, Rudolph, *Mothering* (London: Fontana, 1977).

Schwartz, Pamela M., 'Working Mothers of Infants: Conflicts and Coping Strategies', *Women's Lives* (Ann Arbor: Centre for Women's Studies, 1979).

Seligman, Martin, *Helplessness* (San Francisco: W.H. Freeman, 1975).

Sheehy, Gail, *Passages* (New York: Bantam, 1977).

Sheehy, Gail, *Pathfinders* (New York: William Morrow, 1981).

Spurlock, Jeane, 'Minority Women', presented to the American Psychiatric Association conference on Women's Studies in Psychiatric Education (Washington D.C., 3 December 1981).

Stewart, Wendy Ann, 'A Psychosocial Study of the Formation of the Early Adult Life Structure in Women', doctoral dissertation (New York: Columbia University, 1976).

Stoller, R., 'The "Bedrock" of Masculinity and Femininity: Bisexuality', *Archives of General Psychiatry*, 26 (1972) 207–12.

Stoller, R., 'Overview: The Impact of New Advances in Sex Research on Psychoanalytic Theory', *American Journal of Psychiatry*, 130(3) (1973) 241–51.

Strouse, Jean (ed.), *Women and Analysis* (New York: Grossman Publishers, 1974).

Symonds, Alexandra, 'The Liberated Woman: Healthy and Neurotic', *American Journal of Psychoanalysis*, 34 (1974) 177–83.

Symonds, Alexandra, 'A Neurotic Dependency in Successful Women', *Journal of the American Academy of Psychoanalysis,* 4 (1976) 95–103.

Symonds, Alexandra, 'The Psychodynamics of Expansiveness in the Success-oriented Woman', *American Journal of Psychoanalysis*, 38 (1978) 195–205.

Thompson, Clara, 'The Role of Women in this Culture', *Psychiatry*, 4 (1941) 1–8.

Thompson, Clara, 'Cultural Pressures in the Psychology of Women', *Psychiatry*, 5 (1942).

Thompson, Clara, *On Women* (New York: New American Library, 1971).

Vaillant, George, *Adaptation to Life* (Boston: Little, Brown, 1977).

Wallace, Michele, *Black Macho and the Myth of the Superwoman* (New York: Warner, Books, 1980).

Weissman, M. and G. Klerman, 'Sex Differences and the Epidemiology of Depression', *Archives of General Psychiatry*, 34 (1977) 98–111.

Winnicott, D.W., *The Child, the Family and the Outside World* (Harmondsworth: Penguin, 1964).

Index

Anscombe, Prof. E., 152–3
au pair, 115

Bellows, Carole, 85–6
bonding, x, 51, 177
 see also, dependency needs
Bowlby, John, 46, 47, 48, 49, 52,
  169, 170

career identity, 7
Chodorow, Nancy, 3, 38, 39, 40
Compton, Ann, 94–5

day care, 2, 22, 102, 112, 114, 115,
  181
dependence, 5, 27, 37, 40, 48, 105
dependency needs (attachment), 3,
  5, 6, 8, 10, 19, 44, 48, 83, 92,
  131, 139, 176
depression, 10, 47, 72–83, 99, 175–
  6
Dinnerstein, Dorothy, 39
Dowling, Colette, 7, 30, 121
Drabble, Margaret, 22, 110

Ephron, Nora, 98, 145
expansive needs, 3, 44, 69, 83, 131

fathers, ix, x, 12, 14–26 *passim*, 40,
  44, 50, 51, 58, 138, 145
femininity, 8, 9, 28
feminism, ix, 3, 4, 5, 11, 27, 88,
  145, 149–51, 172, 179
Freud, Sigmund, 36, 37, 38, 47,
  126
Friday, Nancy, 67
Friedan, Betty, 29, 69, 139, 159–60

Garner, Lesley, 161–2
gender identity, 33, 34, 35, 36–40
Gilligan, Carol, 42–4
Graham, Katherine, 67
grandparents, 23, 48, 49
Guest, Judith, 174–5
guilt, 9, 17, 22, 29, 102, 104, 110,
  111

Hennig, Margaret, 138, 139, 140
Hill, Susan, 164–5

193

Hoffman, Mary, 165
Horner, Matina, 63, 64
housekeeper, 15, 22, 48, 49, 115
    see also, nanny, au pair
Hunter, Rita, 67

Ibsen, H., 91–3
independence, 3, 7, 9, 35, 48, 87–
    93, 99, 107, 120, 177

James, Emily*, 84–5, 93–103 *passim*

latchkey children, 114, 116–17
Lazarre, Jane, 157
Leach, Penelope, 46, 49
learned helplessness, 78–83
    see also, fear of success

maternal deprivation, 47–8, 52,
    109, 169, 170
maternal employment, 104–8, 180
    effect on children, 48, 54–60
    see also, motherhood and
        employment
Mitchell, Juliet, 36
motherhood,
    changes in, x, 30, 59
    and employment, 2, 26, 28, 53,
        54, 59, 101, 102, 104–17,
        169–72, 173
    genetic influence in, x, 1, 31, 32,
        33, 52
    importance to women of, 2, 5,
        11, 99
    as institution, 13, 52, 59
mothers and daughters, 3, 6, 8, 24,
    35, 36, 40, 57, 66, 143

nanny, 53, 96, 100, 151, 154
    see also, housekeeper, au pair

O'Reilly, Jane, 25

penis envy, 36, 37
post-feminism, 1, 86
pregnancy, 13, 31
primary parent, 18, 29, 30, 35, 50,
    143

role reversal, 14–26 *passim*
Rossi, Alice, 31
Roth, Philip, 35

Scarf, Maggie, 75, 175–7 *passim*
Scharff, Dr David, 101
Seymour, Lynn, 128–37
Sheehy, Gail, 92
Sills, Beverley, 110–11
single parents, 20, 108
Stiglitz, Joseph E., 16–17, 18–19
Stoller, Robert, 33, 34
success avoidance, 5, 63–71, 106
superwoman syndrome, 9, 10, 29,
    146–51, 155
Symonds, Alexandra, 7, 139

Te Kanawa, Kiri, 124–32
Thatcher, Margaret, 155–8
Thomas, Barbara, 85–6

Wade, Valerie, 107–21 *passim*
Walsh, Julia, 118–21
Walters, Barbara, 70–1, 150
Williams, Shirley, 154–5
Winnicott, D., 13n, 169
Woolf, Virginia, 61